African Co-operatives and Efficiency

AFRICAN CO-OPERATIVES AND EFFICIENCY

EDITED BY

Carl Gösta Widstrand

CONTRIBUTORS:

Yash Ghai, Edward Karanja, M. Lungu, P. Mauremootoo, Shem E. Migot-Adholla, J. L. Murungi, J. J. Musundi, Brown Ngwilulupi, Pheroze Nowrojee, H. Ramdin, Leonora Stettner, C. G. Widstrand

The Scandinavian Institute of African Studies

UPPSALA 1972

The Scandinavian Institute of African Studies has served at Uppsala since 1962 as a Scandinavian documentation and research centre on African affairs.

The views expressed in its publications are entirely those of the authors and do not necessarily reflect those of the Institute or the institutions where they are engaged at present.

ISBN 91-7106-057-X

Printed in Sweden by
Almqvist & Wiksell Informationsindustri AB
Uppsala 1972

Contents

Preface

In April 1970, the Scandinavian Institute of African Studies organized a seminar on "Co-operatives and Rural Development in East Africa". The participants came from Kenya, Tanzania, Uganda and the Scandinavian countries.

The topic was chosen for several reasons. One was the obvious interest in various types of co-operatives as a means of development—economic and egalitarian—that the Governments of Kenya, Tanzania and Uganda have manifested since independence. Another reason was the Scandinavian interest in East Africa in general and especially in the development of co-operatives and co-operative education. A third reason involved the question of tradition—whether the knowledge and experience which the co-operative movements in Scandinavia have amassed over the years would be of any relevance to the co-operatives in East Africa, other than in very general terms. There was also the similar question of whether East African "traditional" co-operative experience was of any relevance to the modern co-operatives in East Africa, other than in very general terms. The papers presented at the seminar and a summary of the discussions have been published. During the seminar it was suggested that the research results of this seminar, especially in the field of efficiency, should be made available to the "movement" in East Africa. It was suggested that the best way of doing this was to organize a follow-up meeting in East Africa, where members of the movement, the co-operative departments and the co-operative educational institutions could meet and discuss recent research findings, as well as suggest new topics for research which they felt should have high priority.

The Scandinavian Institute of African Studies and the East and Central African Office of the International Co-operative Alliance subsequently organized a follow-up seminar entitled "Efficiency in the Performance of Co-operatives", which was held at the Co-operative College, Langata, Kenya, from 29 November to 4 December 1971, with some 40 participants from Botswana, Kenya, Mauritius, Tanzania, Uganda and Zambia. The seminar was jointly financed by the Scandinavian countries through their development assistance organizations.

The papers presented in this volume are the introductory papers sent to the participants before the seminar, as well as the statements made by members of the various organizations participating. A short summary of the proceedings of the seminar and the recommendations of the various committees has been published by the Institute in mimeographed form.

The material in this volume may seem very heterogeneous, but so indeed does the co-operative movement. Moreover, there is another similarity to the co-operatives, although the approaches seem different; the authors of all the papers included here are trying in one way or another to answer the question: "What is co-operative efficiency?"

Finally, I wish to convey the organisers' thanks to the Principal and the staff of the Co-operative College of Kenya for providing such excellent surroundings for the seminar.

Carl Gösta Widstrand

Kapenguria, Kenya, January 1972

C. G. Widstrand

Problems of Efficiency in the Performance of Co-operatives

The purpose of this paper is to provide some topics for discussion concerning the problems of efficiency in co-operatives, such as "Why is efficiency important?" "How does it relate to other goals that co-operatives try to achieve?" and "What factors determine efficiency in co-operatives?"

These are some of the questions to which I shall address myself in this paper. But before proceeding to discuss these questions, let us examine the meaning of the word "efficiency" and how it relates to other concepts like "effectiveness" and "productivity". This may sound theoretical, but I believe that this is where we need to begin.

Why is it necessary to carry on any theoretical discussion to introduce a topic which seems very practical? Why do we need theory? Because we use much theory and because theory guides action. *There is some kind of theory behind every action which a man takes,* as the following example will show.

"Participation" is a concept familiar to all who have been involved in co-operative activities. We may say that the theory behind the concept of "participation in co-operatives" is something like this: "If individuals come together to achieve certain aims in co-operation with others, the participation of all the individuals is necessary fully to achieve these aims." A simple theory like this has several implications. We may derive from it conclusions about the connections between "participation"

Carl Gösta Widstrand is the Director of the Scandinavian Institute of African Studies at Uppsala. He is currently working on the Special Rural Development Programme in Kenya.

and other factors, such as the size of the group of individuals, leadership, etc. But it is more important that *rational patterns of action* may be derived from this theory: in order to get individuals to participate, there must be organization and one must define the goals.

Ideas such as the concepts of egalitarianism, democratic control, and self-help—in other words a kind of ideology—may be found helpful in this context or, indeed, even derive from the theory as a necessary part of the patterns of action. I give this simple and short example of what theory is, in order to show that it is not something which university people sit and brood over in their studies but something which concerns all of us and which we all use.

Simple and Complicated Theories

Admittedly, some theories are more complicated than this one, and therefore more difficult of access. Sometimes they are general, sometimes specific. Sometimes they are also difficult to read, because the language in which scientific theories are expressed has been developed to be precise, which makes it into a very special kind of language.

It is the duty of research workers to "translate" such theories into plain language. There is one very important reason for this. While practical action is guided by some kind of theory, theories that have been suggested must be tested by applying them, that is, by putting them into practice.

To find out whether the theory about "participation" which I mentioned above is useful, we must test it against reality. In operational terms, this may mean, for example, that we choose some co-operatives, try to find a way of assessing "participation"—see how many turn up for meetings and for communal work, ask individuals how they participate, how often and in which way, etc.—and then finally try to compare the performances of co-operatives with "low" and "high" participation. It is indeed also possible for co-operative leaders to get an idea of the degree of participation from these types of observations. I have now given an example of how a grass-roots type of theory can be transformed into ideology and guidance for action, and how active and interested observers can make observations to check a theory that is being put into practice.

Effectiveness and Efficiency

One reason for discussing the ideas of efficiency and effectiveness is that these particular concepts have lately been discussed very much in the literature on administration. There is a difference between the two concepts of *efficiency* and *effectiveness.* Both in theory and in practice, these concepts have been given different contents.

Effectiveness is the word generally used in discussing results in combination with the means of achieving such results, against the background of the *aims* and *goals* of the activity. Such aims may be expected or real. A co-operative movement is effective when it brings about the general aims of co-operation in a country. This may mean getting more and more people into the movement, in order to benefit from the movement, and getting more and more people to embrace the ideas of co-operation and the "spirit" (however defined) of co-operation. The aim, for example, of the *Ujamaa* movement is

> ... to build a society in which all members have equal rights and equal opportunities; in which all can live at peace with his neighbours without suffering or imposing injustice, being exploited or exploiting; and in which all have a gradually increasing basic level of material welfare before any individual lives in luxury.[1]

Ujamaa co-operative organisation is *effective* when this aim is achieved. The effectiveness of a co-operative is thus the degree to which it fulfils the aims, as they have been set for the movement. It is, however, not always easy to define the aims of a movement or of a public agency such as the co-operative movement in other than very general terms. There are factors that cannot be measured; success or failure often cannot be quantified—they cannot be expressed in numbers or figures but have to be assessed in other ways.

Efficiency is closely associated with the idea of productivity, that is, the relation between the results or achievements and the costs or sacrifices needed to achieve the results. In other words, the volume of effort is related to the costs. In mathematical terms, this means the relationships between input and output and between cost and benefit.

The smaller the margin between the two, the more efficient an economic organization is. In other words, if a co-operative society handles members' produce, allowing for only a 15% deduction for administration, transport and fixed commissions, it is more efficient than a society which needs to make a 25% deduction for the same purpose. In handling the produce, the former society has consumed less of the value of the produce. When we talk about efficiency, therefore, we are concerned about reducing the "overhead" costs, the amount of money the society spends in handling the produce. In Kenya, co-operative societies are not expected to spend more than 20% on administration, transport and commissions, but very few societies manage to hit this target.

A similar situation exists in the other East African countries. The fact that farmers often do not get any obvious economic benefits from being members of co-operative societies, compared with non-members or the private market, is a main reason for the dissatisfaction with many of these co-operative societies. Thus, it is important that problems of efficiency and the question of how performance can be improved should be discussed. Most of this paper will be devoted to this discussion.

Better Performance of the Wrong Tasks

It is, however, necessary to remember the difference between effectiveness and efficiency: effectiveness is always assessed against a superior aim or goal. A one-sided interest in efficiency problems (productivity) may result in "a better performance of the wrong tasks". It is possible to be efficient without being effective. A co-operative may be economically efficient, but if—as has happened—only a minority of the co-operators profit from the economic efficiency, then the co-operative is not effective.

One common reason for this is that no clear goal has been defined or that there are competing goals within the co-operative. Sometimes, where the goals and objectives are well defined, there has been a less than whole-hearted acceptance of these goals by the members. The co-operatives must seek support from their members, both by providing the essential services *and* by incorporating their requirements in their current goals.[2]

Shem Migot-Adholla has made a study of some aspects of the *distribution and handling of tractors* in Maswa district in Sukumaland. In the allocation of the scarce resources, there was a difference of opinion between the administrative staff and the more politically motivated committee members as to whether the goal was social accountability or economically efficient performance. That is, the staff wanted to maximise the productivity of the tractors, for example, by planning their use, in order to avoid travelling far in different directions every morning. The committee members, however, wanted to have the social prestige of deciding who was to be offered the tractor services, disregarding the question of economic efficiency. Neither of the goals was wholly fulfilled, and the co-operative was not effective.[3]

The Feldmans have shown from Nduli in Tanzania that a certain type of co-operative organization was modestly efficient in the *growing and handling of tobacco* but that the ecological problems and the special problems with the crop (plus the capitalistic tendencies among the small farmers) destroyed the larger initial co-operative.[4] Many co-operatives established for administrative convenience are sometimes not effective in this sense, even though they are fairly efficient, as people do not feel any co-operative "spirit" (participation!).

Effectiveness is crucial to the success of the concept of *Ujamaa*. The goal is to create an egalitarian socialist society, and the *Ujamaa* co-operatives will not be effective unless this is what their members are striving for all the time. The goal takes a long time to achieve, but it is necessary that effectiveness should not be jeopardized by over-zealous implementation and demands for rigid conformity that may stifle efficiency and local initiative, which are crucial to success. The extent of voluntary commitment to this new system is also crucial in determining the degree of success or failure, so that the movement does not degenerate into another bureaucracy with no local initiative.[5]

Efficiency is, of course, necessary in order to achieve the long-term goal of *Ujamaa*. But *Ujamaa* villages also have to be efficient, in order to show that socialism in this form can pay in the short term. The partial goal against which effectiveness can then be measured is the ability of the *Ujamaa* movement to show that it is the right and indeed only option.

Another Way of Looking at Effectiveness

I have already said that there is great difficulty in defining the aims of a co-operative. To define the aims and goals of such an institution or those of a ministry, a department of community development, a department of health or even a hospital is not easy. The current discussion on the aims of an organization is based on the problems of private enterprises, but some of the ideas may also be helpful in discussing the effectiveness of public or government activity and in connection with effectiveness in co-operatives.

One of the points that has been made is that it is useful to divide the aims of an organization into two sets of objectives:

(*a*) The objectives *of* an organization, that is, the function of the organization in society (which may be to provide services of various types, as is the case with the co-operatives), and

(*b*) The objectives *for* an organization, that is, its aims, based on the ideas, feelings and opinions of groups or individuals connected with the organization (who in the case of co-operatives may be the members, committee members, staff, government co-operative officers, etc.). These people are very often outside the main organization itself (non-members, but also the members in a large union) and constitute a group with many different ideas and many different ways of expressing these ideas and pressing for their realization.

In a situation like this, we speak today of *internal* (or inner) and *external* (or outer) effectiveness. Some factors affect the outer, others the inner effectiveness. The interested parties decide what kind of influence one may exert on the organization (or tolerate from the organization). *Outer effectiveness* is

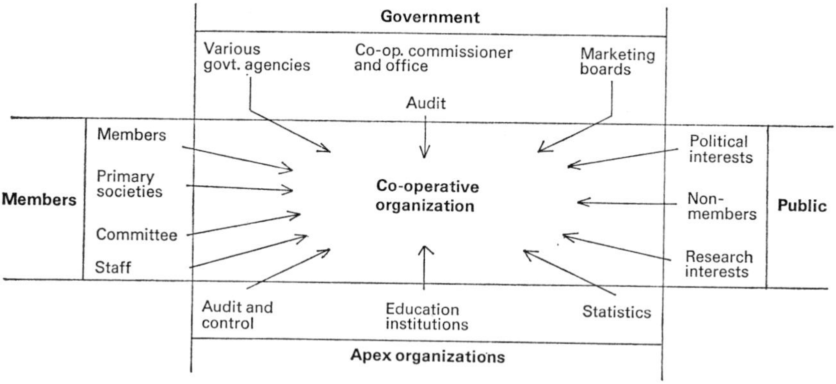

Fig. 1.

thus the way in which the organization has managed to fulfil the expectations of the interested parties. *Inner effectiveness,* in its turn, means the use of the resources of production within the organization to fulfil operationally formulated goals within the organization. Efficiency and productivity would in this case be subordinate to the concept of inner effectiveness, and a means of achieving inner effectiveness.

Inner effectiveness in a co-operative union would mean that it achieves the goal of a certain output and, in order to do so, accepts or organizes opportunities for more primary societies to join. The outer effectiveness of the organization is decided in terms of the aims which the different interested parties ("pressure groups") would like to see fulfilled by the co-operative union. The members would like more returns, the committee members more power, the government more control, and the apex organization has its own ideas of what aims and goals should be formulated for the union.

In the case of a co-operative organization, the different groups and parties that have an interest in the organization and also different views on its main goals may be illustrated as in Fig. 1. Sometimes influential groups (such as the government and sometimes the members) manage to get their own ideas about the effectiveness of the union made "official" by political action. The problem of partly conflicting objectives is fundamental to economics and to administration, yet its practical implications have only recently begun to concern planners.

In this connection it may be noted that, unlike the co-operatives in Europe, when they were set up in the last century, marketing co-operatives in Africa today are expected to promote a large number of diffuse goals and their activities are not focussed on social betterment alone. They are not responsible to the members only, as were the European co-operatives, but are equally dependent on outside interests, sometimes governmental, sometimes private.

Effectiveness has to be assessed against a goal, progress towards effectiveness against partial goals. Very often there are no exact or clearly defined goals. In that case, the assessment of the effectiveness becomes very difficult. Often several groups have different ideas about the goals of an organization like a co-operative. They will then have different views of what is meant by effectiveness.

Problems of Efficiency, As Seen by Co-operative Staff and Members

In two recent works on co-operatives in East Africa, the members, staff and committee members were asked for their opinions on various topics concerned with efficiency and co-operatives. In a Kenya study the question was asked: "Which is the more important for a co-operative union—that it is economically efficient or that it is democratically controlled?" Exactly two-thirds of all the respondents answered: "Economically efficient" (75% of the staff, 72% of the committee members).[6]

In a Uganda study by E. Brett, members were asked whether their co-operatives were working better or worse now than at the time of joining. Only a small majority (54%) felt that the co-operatives were now working better, whereas 19% answered "Same", and 26% thought that they were functioning "Worse". Almost half of the members also thought that the co-operatives were run by the Government and not by the members.[7]

The Kenya study also inquired into the different notions of efficiency and what it really was. To the question "What criteria have to be fulfilled before a union can be considered efficient?", there was a variety of answers. Some 17% (all of them committee members) regarded efficiency as a problem associated with the quality of staff: "When we have trained staff", "If we have honest staff", "When employees work hard". Others claimed that a union was efficient "when its books were in order".

Forty-two per cent regarded the matter as being determined by the relationship between the committee and the staff: "When harmony exists between committee and staff", "When the staff obeys the committee", "When committee members and staff work well together", "When all are united". Twenty-eight per cent thought that environmental factors determined efficiency. Quite a few said that efficiency could only be achieved "if primary societies are financially sound". Others referred to the middleman as an obstacle to co-operative efficiency. A few thought that efficiency could only be achieved if farming was carried out on a large-scale basis. Only 4% mentioned that the most important proof of efficiency was a "maximum return to the members".[6]

I now want to discuss some of the problems raised by the answers to the questions on efficiency put in the above-mentioned surveys. These questions refer to such matters as efficiency and the social environment of co-operatives, efficiency and scale, size and participation, efficiency and democratic control, efficiency and staff and management problems, efficiency and co-operative education, and efficiency and government control. Most of these matters are relevant both to marketing co-operatives and to producers' co-operatives, though I shall not mention this explicitly each time. I shall not discuss consumers' co-operatives.

Efficiency and the Social Environment of Co-operatives

Social factors play an important role in the efficiency of management of co-operatives, so let me begin by discussing them. A major problem is the character of peasant society itself. Contrary to what so many African leaders have said, traditional communalism has turned out to be more of a liability than an asset to modern co-operative development. The rural face-to-face group that ordinarily lives and works together is too small to form the basis of a modern co-operative. When incorporated into a larger structure, together with other similar groups, it proves its basic inflexibility. Inside the co-operative society, these often self-contained social units become involved in factional warfare over the control of co-operative resources and their distribution. This means that parochial rather than technical or economic considerations tend to determine the outcome of management decisions.

The stratification of rural society. A further major problem is that, although it has already become stratified economically, the peasant society is still only just starting to move out from under the dominance of clan and extended family relationships. There has developed over the years a gap between the rural bourgeoisie or the economic activists among the peasants, on the one hand, and the "traditional" farmers, on the other. Yet this latter group have not developed any consciousness of their own situation as an exploited group but still attach great importance to clan and family relationships. Their closest allies are still not peasants in the same economic position but relatives of various kinds.

One may elaborate this as a difference between "horizontal" and "vertical" relationships: the horizontal relationships are relationships between people in the same economic position, while the vertical relationships are between individuals in various positions of economic power, either informal relationships, such as patron–client relationships, or dependent relationships, such as creditor–debtor relationships, or formal relationships, i.e. individuals belonging to the same cultural group, clan, lineage or family. Very often there is a combination of all three types. The category of vertical relationships includes

> ... teachers, priests, traders, administrators and politicians. They often get into leading positions, because the ordinary peasants believe them to be more able to defend the interests of the local community than they are themselves. The peasants give them full support in return for the favours or rewards that they can secure from the "outside world". Co-operatives in East Africa are thus very often ruled on the basis of already existing informal "patron–client" relationships.
>
> The importance of this "vertical" relationship is re-enforced by the fact that social ties based on kinship and other local institutions are still more important than the mutual loyalty between peasants in different village communities. The "horizontal" ties of economic interest have not yet replaced the "vertical" ties of social obligation based on such units as the clan, village, etc.[8]

Co-operatives have therefore to date been unable to modify existing economic inequalities. The poor peasant with insufficient means to support and educate his family prefers to enter into a client relationship with one of the richer members of his community rather than to challenge the existing system. Attempts by urban, ideologically committed leaders to put an end to these patron–client relationships have met with little success.

Because of their social dependence on the co-operative leaders and because of sheer ignorance, ordinary peasant-members do not exercise any democratic control over the management of the co-operatives. For instance, the balance sheet read to them at the annual general meeting is beyond the comprehension of most members attending the meeting.

Traditional ideas about co-operation and efficiency. A further problem in the same group is that it has been generally believed that "traditional" co-operative action, usually based on family or clan relationships (such as common house-building, weeding, path clearance, etc.), could be used as a basis for creating modern co-operatives. Indeed, this is one of the basic ideas in the *Ujamaa* movement. Such notions may be used as an ideology of traditionalism and succeed politically, as indeed they seem to have done in the case of *Ujamaa*. But it is not advisable to rely very heavily on the pre-existent socialism of the "traditional" society.[8] Traditional communal groups are based on the exclusion of others not belonging to the same family clan; to "us", modern co-operatives are rather based on the inclusion of everyone who wants to be and has the capacity to be a member.

Thus, many scholars who try to specify what it is that makes the African peasant "tick" tend to treat him as some exotic social type, characterised by basic benevolence and by being relatively undifferentiated. But these assumptions do not obtain in reality. Socio-economic differentiation and kinship–neighbourhood loyalties are important among the factors affecting participation by individuals in the co-operative organization. At the same time, other variables, such as ecology, transportation and the availability of a market for agricultural goods, affect the development of co-operatives. Many of these factors clearly did not pertain under the traditional system. In addition, they represented an expansion of the scale of the activities in which the African peasants are involved today. These factors alone point to the fact that there is no direct continuity between the "traditional" co-operative forms and modern marketing co-operatives.[8]

Obviously, the simple apposition of "vertical" and "horizontal" is an absurd over-simplification. Traditional societies had both horizontal and vertical organization (age-sets in Africa, caste in India). Moreover, the *form* of vertical organization differs greatly in particular traditional societies; for these particulars, the advice of the (currently rather neglected) anthropologists is needed. In most cases, we are not dealing with "pure" traditional societies, but with farming communities who have already had considerable contact both with the money economy and with the political systems which have grown up with independence. It is probably very widely true to say that the amalgam of persistent elements of tradition (extended family, clan, etc.) with new forms of influence (local politicians, commerce, the possibility of receiving benefits from government programmes) has led to vertical, patronage relationships *in the present phase,* far more than to "horizontal" economic relationships, which cut across family, clan, caste or traditional hierarchies.[9]

I may sum up all this by saying that traditional societies with a fairly strong vertical type of social organization, which have already developed elements of "modern" leadership, will tend to absorb co-operatives into this style of life (patronage, segmentary competition, etc.). In consequence, co-operatives will tend to re-emphasize and strengthen social stratification. The egalitarian and socialist aims of co-operatives may thus be, at least partially and temporarily, frustrated and thus also their effectiveness.

Efficiency and Scale, Size and Participation

A somewhat confused issue lies concealed in the arguments concerning efficiency, size and participation. The arguments for size in primary societies and for building unions and federations on top of primary societies are usually put forward on grounds of efficiency—larger funds, better services to members, more power in the market, and so on. However, while some marketing and processing operations need considerable size if they are to be economic,

> effective organization and effective participation are governed by the rule of optimal size, as well as the processing of tea or coffee. Effective participation decreases sharply with increasing membership.[9]

There are three points here. *First,* the relation between size and participation, *second,* the fact that large size requires professional managerial ability, and, *third,* the fact that, whereas the initial reason for starting co-operatives is usually to provide a primary grouping of many individual farmers (for the sake of extension and credit services, and for sharing some kind of facility—tractor, pump, dairy, etc.), once this primary grouping is achieved, the higher, large-scale functions can just as well be done either commercially or by a semi-public corporation. Is the *primary* object of co-operatives to encourage participation and to provide a grouping of a few score of individual farmers or is it to create an organization capable of competing, in managerial efficiency and in rewards to the growers, with a commercial enterprise? Too often, co-operative marketing organizations end up with a six-storey building and low prices to producers.

The interest of employees is partly in preserving the size of their hierarchy and, if need be, expanding it, and, of course, in better conditions and pay for themselves. This is quite contrary to the interests of the farmer.[9]

In the Uganda Inquiry Report of 1967, it is stated that the largest co-operative unions are the worst managed and that a smaller size of the co-operative unions is desirable. In Tanzania, attempts have been made more recently to create region-wide co-operative unions. When such a regional amalgamation was achieved in Arusha, it was hailed as a victory for the peasants.

Which is the more desirable—a small or a big union? The answer is, of course, that both have their merits and demerits and their costs and benefits. These will vary from place to place, depending on the scope of the activities assigned to the co-operatives, the members' ability to take advantage of large-scale operations, the economic foundation of the co-operatives, etc. It is clear, for instance, that, if co-operative unions function well and can purchase fertilizers and other goods centrally for the farmers on a wholesale basis at a much cheaper rate than if each society placed its own orders, there is an economic advantage in having large unions. At the same time, however, control of the organization is further removed from the members; the union becomes a more autonomous organization and will only benefit the farmers if the union leaders and staff are efficient and honest. If this is not the case, the disadvantages of large unions will tend to prevail. Members will become disillusioned and society leaders disloyal to their own union. Thus, efficiency does not come automatically from amalgamating smaller organizations into larger ones.[2]

All this suggests that the problems of running large-scale and complex economic organizations do not lend themselves very readily to solution by decisions taken at annual meetings composed of poorly educated and badly informed members. Furthermore, what is often gained in economy of scale by centralizing is lost in the maintenance of secondary societies and in political manoeuvring to control the union resources.

Efficiency and Democratic Control

There is a frequent discrepancy between the size of the economically viable unit and the socially acceptable unit. This problem leads us to another aspect which should be discussed here—how control is exercised in co-operatives, to ensure honesty and efficiency on the part of the management. This question needs to be looked at on two levels, as it is a problem of size. First, it needs to be discussed in relation to the control of primary societies and, secondly, to control at the union level.

At the primary-society level in marketing co-operatives and on the *Ujamaa* level, the co-operative operates on the basis of all the members being eligible to attend general meetings and to vote in elections. E. Brett remarks that, in Uganda, participation at this level seems to be relatively extensive and this is certainly also true of the other East African countries. Eighty-eight per cent of Brett's sample claimed that they had attended a meeting at some time or another, and more than half claimed fairly regular attendance.[7]

Union democracy. On the union level the problem of democratic control may be looked at somewhat differently. We must remember that, in any organization, management is a struggle for power and control between the various groups or cliques participating in it. In co-operatives, it may be between the members and the staff or between various factions in the committee itself. But participation in itself is not a simple measure of democratic control. It is not until the members themselves feel a sense of involvement and have some control over the co-operative (through education, involvement in production activities, understanding the proceedings, etc.) that efficiency can be guaranteed by pressure from below, by active participation by the membership.

The difficult problem here is how to maximise the requisite active participation by the members and ultimately enable the movement to wield such pressure. One of the problems in this respect is that it is not unusual to have one farmer belonging to more than four different co-operative societies at the same time. In such circumstances, it is a big burden for such a farmer to participate actively in every one of these single-purpose co-operative societies.[2] This is particularly so, as each committee member is regarded as representing a specific geographical area (in some cases, perhaps a special clan or tribe). The committee member, as the representatives of a group of self-sufficient farmers, is primarily concerned with demonstrating his ability to secure benefits for his "constituents". He is expected to secure for his supporters as many benefits and rewards as possible. At the same time, he can usually obtain personal privileges. His supporters would not object to this practice, as long as he helps them to satisfy their needs; the latter may be collective, for example, the building of a new coffee factory, or individual, for example, paying school fees, obtaining a loan to buy a new graded cow, etc. Thus, even if he does secure benefits for his "constituents" through illegal operations, they will not necessarily object. The law matters much less than the goods obtained.

We can see, therefore, that members and their representatives on the management committee or board are more concerned with the control of resources than their efficient use. There is in most marketing co-operatives an inherent conflict between business efficiency and control by local groups. In this situation, it is not surprising that the tug-of-war between those who want to improve the business efficiency of co-operatives (particularly the government departments responsible for co-operatives) and those who want to control their resources is a main feature of the co-operative scene in eastern Africa.

The political aspect of co-operatives. We also have to accept that, in each attempt to change the character of co-operative management, there will be some who will promote it and others who will oppose it (either directly or indirectly). What is an advantage to some is a disadvantage to others. We cannot disregard the "political" aspect of co-operatives. What we can do, perhaps, is to manage these political conflicts so that they do not damage the co-operative organizations extensively.

Efficiency, Management and Staff Problems

References to co-operative-management inefficiency are common in the whole of East Africa. Under this general heading fall a substantial number of problems: corruption and deliberate misuse of funds, "bureaucratization" and excessive overhead costs, improper use of staff, lack of commitment to the society, and insufficient control over the management.

Corruption. Corruption and the deliberate misuse of funds is the most serious of the many management problems facing co-operatives. The reason for the high incidence of corruption or fraud cases in the co-operative movement seems to be the conflict of standards and norms implied in the formal regulations of co-operatives and the informal customs prevailing in the rural areas. Though it would be going too far to defend, unconditionally, corrupt practices in the co-operative movement, there is something in Migot-Adholla's suggestion that "some amount of 'slip' is necessary in any organization, to stimulate interest and thus encourage efficiency". At the same time, however, it is clear that corruption, if allowed to spread, gives rise to other types of inefficiency.

The *Tanzania Committee of Enquiry* into the co-operatives also took a strong stand against corruption:

With regret we must report that, in a great many cases, society secretaries engage in petty thievery, often in collaboration with a corrupt committeeman, and sometimes not so petty (1966).

The *Uganda Inquiry Report* of 1967 has the following to say:

There is a tendency among members, board (committee) members, and managers to use union lorries as their own property. Members feel that the lorries belong to them, and therefore they are entitled to a free ride. It was alleged that, at one time in Bugisu, union transport used to go and collect board members from their homes to attend board meetings and take them back after the meeting.

Excessive bureaucracy and poor and rigid management. If misappropriation of union and society money and assets is common practice in all three countries, heavy overhead costs due to poor and rigid management practices is another. In a speech at the Co-operative College, Moshi, the Minister for Finance and Administration in the East African Community admitted that it still remained a serious problem that the farmer did not get the prices that it was thought he would get after the middleman had been eliminated. He attributed the failure to the "bureaucratic organization of the co-operative movement" (*Daily Nation,* 4 November 1970). He went on to say that societies had been filling jobs because there were vacancies to be filled, without considering the administrative costs involved.

The same attitude towards the co-operative society as an employment-creating institution that we found in Kenya seems to prevail also in Tanzania and Uganda. One observer of a coffee co-operative society in south-western Tanzania shows how much of the power struggle in the committee was over the questions of who should be employed and how the employment opportunities should be distributed.[10] The Uganda Inquiry Report mentions, as one of the causes of poor management, the fact that many unions are too big in relation to the availability of trained, experienced, local staff.

Both the Ugandan and the Tanzanian Report looked very seriously at the manpower situation in the co-operative movement. The Uganda Report laments that many persons would like to take up an honest career with the co-operatives but are thwarted by the unbridled machinations of committee members, some of whom have a vested interest in retaining their posts. It was apparent to the members of the Committee of Inquiry that there was no security for the employees; many of them did not possess any service agreements and could be dismissed summarily. The Tanzanian Report emphasizes a similar staff problem when it says that employees do not regard themselves as a professional group, with ethical standards to live up to, with career possibilities and with opportunities for promotion to situations of greater responsibility. On the contrary, the Report continues, they generally feel that they are at the mercy of uninformed and sometimes corrupt committeemen, who have the unrestrained power to employ, fix the terms of service, and discharge all employees of the co-operatives (pp. 10–11).

It must be added here, however, that the organization in Tanzania of a Unified Co-operative Service Commission, as the result of the Report of the Commission of Inquiry, will probably solve many of the problems concerned with careers in the co-operatives.

At times, however, the roles are reversed and a too-clever employee feels free to run the committee, playing on his literacy and greater knowledge, and secure against control by others. One example of this is when secretaries tell ordinary members that the price of a certain crop has fallen, when in fact it remains the same. Under these circumstances, provided the uninformed members do not discover the fraud, the employee can make significant amounts of money, capitalizing on the ignorance of the members.[11]

The problem of loyalty. This brings us to the question of *loyalty.* It is understandable if staff tend to be disloyal to their employers, given the unpleasant conditions under which they are often asked to work. It is more serious when the members themselves are not loyal. We noted that "outside interests" impinge upon co-operatives. Committee members in Uganda have often acted with their personal interests in mind, disregarding what is best for their organization. The *Official Committee of Inquiry into the Busoga Growers' Co-operative Union, Ltd.* (1966) says:

The cause of this colossal loss (more than two million Shs in 1962–3) was masterly inactivity and gross irresponsibility by everyone concerned with the Union, from the Committee down to the ginnery manager. No employee had the common sense or initiative to take remedial action to prevent bales of cotton being damaged by rain, for fear of incurring the displeasure of the Committee (1966, p. 27).

Cultural problems. Tribal sentiments have also affected and determined management performance in various co-operative organizations in Uganda. The same problem has been recorded in Tanzania. McHenry illustrates this in his study of the fishermen's co-operative on the shores of Lake Tanganyika.[12] The problem there was that the fishermen, who were scattered along many miles of the shoreline, were brought together into a single society. The head office was established at the commercial centre of the industry (Kigoma). The branches were organized at the major fishing centres along the lake. The geographical distance to the society office encouraged disloyalty on the part of members, who argued that they should at each branch be allowed to register their own society. This move would enhance loyalty and encourage the fishermen to boost their society. Such a move, however, was never agreed to by the political and co-operative leadership. Thus, one contributory factor to the failure to organize this fishermen's society was these endless disputes between the head office and the branches.

Apathy among members. Poor management often leads to apathy among the members. They show no interest in the affairs of their society. Thus, it is important in every society that at least a reasonably good level of management should be maintained.

Moreover, there seems to be a tendency in many societies for poor management to become worse, once it has begun. Poor management often discourages members and also makes them less interested in their society. As a result of this, committee members and staff get even more opportunities to mismanage the society. This vicious circle can usually only be broken by government supervision, but, due to lack of staff and delayed auditing, financial irregularities are often discovered much too late, when they have already had an adverse effect on the members.

Efficiency and Co-operative Education

One way of getting around this problem of sloppy management has been to intensify co-operative-education efforts. But how important is *education* for promoting efficiency? It is generally assumed that co-operative-management education is one of the most effective tools for improving performance in co-operatives. To a considerable extent this is, of course, true. Increased understanding of management principles does help both the committee member and the secretary of a primary society.

But, again, it must be remembered that the realities of co-operative management in the rural areas of eastern Africa are often widely different from the ones to which the co-operator is exposed in a co-operative training course. The factional warfare in the committee and the lack of trust existing between committee members and staff often make it impossible to practise the principles learnt during training courses.

Moreover, there is a danger of placing too heavy an emphasis on education. Many employees in co-operatives get automatic promotion or a salary increase after having completed a particular training course. The employee does not have to prove his increased value to the organization. It is taken for granted that the course itself makes him so much more valuable that the co-operative should give him a better status or a higher income. It may be desirable, however, from the point of view of efficiency to relate salary increases and promotion to achievements in the organization. If a person works hard and the output increases as a result of it, he should be given encouragement in the form of better payment or promotion. He must increase his contribution to the co-operative before the latter offers him anything in return. This would be one way of improving efficiency, as any salary increase is then directly related to increased output.

Efficiency and Government Control

How does increasing the government supervision and regulation of co-operatives affect efficiency? It is clear in Kenya, Tanzania and Uganda that the Co-operative Societies Act, introduced during the last few years, has had the effect of reducing the most serious cases of mismanagement and misappropriation of funds. The "laissez-faire" period, immediately after independence, has been replaced by a strong control exercised by the Co-operative Departments. In this way money has been saved in the co-operative movement and the ordinary member can feel a bit more certain that his money is not being misused.

But the new regulations have caused other difficulties which tend to affect efficiency. The close government control now exercised has given the members the impression that the co-operative is not theirs. It is just another government organization. Commitment among members and leaders, therefore, is low in most places.

When the government has pressed or forced a co-operative upon a peasant community which has not asked for one, the alienated membership may react with indifference and apathy and with a feeling that they cannot influence the decisions about their own co-operative and about their own future. The creation of co-operatives by the government for administrative convenience is likely to negate active democratic participation, and may (particularly in the case of settlements) produce attitudes of dependence or apathy. This is particularly likely to happen if there is no clear, tangible benefit around which the co-operative is built.[9]

Dependence on outside agents. Another negative effect is that co-operatives have become increasingly accountable to an outside agent (the Co-operative Department) rather than to their own members. This means, for instance, that staff and leaders have to spend many hours every week just filling in the forms which are part of the machinery through which the government controls these co-operatives. This system of management control has not been internalized and is regarded in most co-operatives more as an extra burden than a positive tool for controlling the management process. It is probably true that these measures are necessary at this stage of co-operative development, but it must be remembered that they imply certain costs and the sooner they can be replaced by other means of improving management control which are internal to the co-operative movement itself, the better. One way, which must still be considered in the long-term perspective, is improved understanding of co-operative management among the members. When the members can constitute a genuine source of control, this will be an effective substitute for the present government-imposed system of management control and will save money for the government, as a Co-operative Department is an expensive affair, even if the fees are squeezed out of the co-operatives.

Acknowledgements

In the preparation of this paper, I have profited very much from discussions with members of the co-operative movements and government co-operative staff in Kenya, Mauritius, Tanzania, Uganda and Zambia during journeys in 1970 and 1971. I am also very indebted to Göran Hydén, of the University of Dar-es-Salaam, and to Rune Forsberg, of the ICA Regional Office, Moshi, for comments, ideas and criticism.

Leonora Stettner

Research Priorities in East Africa in Relation to Co-operative Efficiency

In recent years, there has been an upsurge of active interest on the part of research workers in the effectiveness of co-operatives as instruments of development in the less-advanced countries of the world. At least three major events are worth noting in this connection: a seminar on "Social Prerequisites for Agricultural Co-operation" held at the Institute of Development Studies, Sussex University, in April 1969; the seminar on "Co-operatives and Rural Development in East Africa" held by the Scandinavian Institute of African Studies in Uppsala in May 1970, the papers of which have been published under the same title; and the commissioning by the U.N. Research Institute for Social Development in Geneva of several volumes of case studies and analytical appraisals of co-operatives in Latin America, Africa and Asia. The U.N.R.I.S.D. studies were prepared by university scholars, primarily sociologists, and four of the six volumes have already been published.

This awakening of interest is very much to be welcomed by co-operators, and particularly by research workers in the movement and in U.N. agencies like the I.L.O. and the F.A.O., which have long been active in relation to co-operatives in developing countries. Without doubt, they all agree that the usefulness of co-operative research can be greatly enhanced by cross-fertilization of ideas with social scientists in academic circles.

Mrs. L. Stettner is the Secretary for Research at the International Co-operative Alliance in London.

The International Co-operative Alliance attaches top priority to the exchange of information, research and ideas among co-operators, researchers and educators. Moreover we are convinced that this exchange is crucial to the success of the effort to promote co-operative development in the less-advanced areas of the world. Our reasons for believing this are outlined in a paper which was presented by the I.C.A. Secretary for Research to the Third International Conference on Aid to Co-operatives in Developing Countries, held in Loughborough, England, in April 1971. That paper also sketches, in a very general way which is applicable to all developing countries, some of the broad problem areas in which we feel further research is required in order to determine the objectives and priorities for co-operative development. The purpose of the following paper is to pinpoint the subject of this seminar by suggesting specific problems in East Africa which seem to require further research.

The list is not comprehensive, and it may be that the priorities are wrong. Moreover almost every one of the proposed areas for research overlaps two or more of the others which are listed. Thus, there is wide scope for defining the precise framework of individual studies within these broad proposals. The intention in putting forth these suggestions is not to close the subject but rather to be provocative, in the sense of stimulating a lively exchange of views as to what the research priorities should be in this part of the developing world.

Organisational Structure of Co-operatives

Should the major promotional effort be concentrated on primary societies or on secondary servicing organisations? On production co-operatives, credit co-operatives, supply co-operatives, marketing co-operatives or multi-purpose co-operative societies? How much support should be given to pre- or para-co-operative groupings which do not yet qualify as fully fledged co-operatives? What structure would prove most conducive to democratic control and a free flow of information and communication between the various levels?

The appropriate scale of operations necessarily depends on the type of production or commercial activity, the existing patterns of labour co-operation and land tenure, the availability of raw materials, capital, management and technical skills, and other social and economic factors. Hence both intensive and extensive research is required in order to collect the empirical data needed for a determination of the appropriate technology and scale of operations.

Co-operative Efficiency

Social stratification. Research in East Africa has already pointed to the problems of "élitism" and "factionalism" within co-operatives as a result of traditional kinship, clan or tribal ties combined with economic and social inequalities. One result has been the emergence of a few privileged "leaders" of the community—traders, moneylenders, wealthy farmers or landowners, politicians—who exercise undue influence over the affairs of co-operatives, and appropriate an undue share of the fruits of the joint enterprise. Meanwhile the rest of the members apathetically accept the decisions of the few and fail to develop an individual initiative or drive towards self-help and democratic control which would qualify them as genuine co-operators. Further research is required to establish the dimensions of this problem, which has come to be known as the "patron–client relationship", and to provide the basis for tackling it, presumably on the educational and administrative fronts.

Motivation. A closely related problem concerns the difficulty of imbuing members with a sense of involvement. This is partly a matter of combatting the traditional tendency referred to above to accept unquestioningly the "guidance" of social or economic or tribal leaders. It is also an educational or communication problem of convincing members that it is possible for them by their own efforts to improve their situation. This implies a search for specific ways of demonstrating the short-run perceptible benefits from co-operation, of providing members with tangible incentives to increased effort, perhaps through bonuses or differential rewards according to performance, and of assuring them that they are working for themselves and that they can exercise freedom of discussion and of decision. Various devices to these ends have been experimented with, and a thorough investigation and compilation should be attempted on the basis of case studies and analytical evaluations.

Management. Efficient management is recognised as a major factor in the economic viability of co-operatives, and research to date has revealed serious deficiencies in this respect. In large part, the answer is considered to lie in management training, which is discussed below. Nevertheless, there are a number of other pertinent factors which could well be looked at more carefully by researchers. These include stricter safeguards against corruption (both in its petty and its more virulent manifestations), incentive bonuses based on "performance" criteria (which have yet to be developed), higher salaries, improved career structures, and relations between full-time managers and committee members.

Democratic control. Perhaps the first problem to which researchers might address themselves in this connection is the definition of "co-operative efficiency". If the co-operative principle of democracy has any meaning, then "efficiency" must imply not only maximum output (however defined) but also the kinds of output and the distribution of the yield from that output which reflect the democratically expressed wishes of members. Thus, careful study must be given to ways of combatting "élitism" and "factionalism" within co-operative committees, to member and staff education and to making sure that co-operative administrative machinery and co-operative legislation are geared to effective democratic control.

Education. The educational structure in some African countries is a handicap to the development process, in that it is too academic, literary and theoretical in content and not sufficiently related to the practical work and lives for which most of the students should be preparing. Much more serious is the fact that only a small proportion of the population have access to educational opportunities, and that the majority are illiterate. Thus, the system caters for the élite, both in content and in availability, thereby perpetuating inequality.

Co-operative enterprise is highly dependent upon competent management and trained staff, and these are extremely scarce under an educational system like that just described. Lack of practical training and attitudes inimical to manual work make it difficult for co-operatives to recruit adequate personnel. This has accounted for a high percentage of the co-operative failures to date.

Co-operatives can do a great deal to supplement basic education and to help people retain literacy skills once acquired. Through educational programmes for members and on-the-job training, they can build up a corps of skilled workers and competent administrative and managerial staff—but only if these people have already been given an opportunity by the public authorities to acquire literacy skills and rational attitudes to work.

Thus, co-operative researchers could well concern themselves with the public educational facilities in East Africa and examine the possibilities of achieving a more even distribution as between social classes, the sexes, and urban and rural areas; a better balance as between facilities for primary, secondary and higher education; more training for adults; expansion of the teacher-training programmes and an increase of teachers' salaries; and changes to ensure that the content of education is more practical and work-oriented.

Also attention should be given to co-operative experiments in functional education and on-the-job training, preparation of appropriate co-operative educational materials and audio-visual aids and programmes at the village level (for example, a system of rural *animateurs*) designed to stimulate the local population to discuss their problems and to seek group solutions to them.

Technical and advisory services. In addition to greatly expanded facilities for training of management, staff and members, primary societies in East Africa are clearly in need of an extensive network of expert technical, advisory and servicing facilities at the operating level. These include co-operative extension services; specialist advice on accounting, purchasing and marketing; instruction on productive techniques; access to collective facilities, such as transport, storage and machinery; centralised provision of specific phases of processing; banking and credit facilities; joint research institutes;

centres for specialised market and industry information; guidance in preparing loan applications, etc. Thus, there is an urgent need of research on existing and potential facilities for providing such services and possible ways of obtaining the necessary expertise and financial support.

The Influence of Governments on Co-operative Efficiency

The complex problem of relationships between co-operatives and governments is particularly crucial in East Africa, where governments are giving strong support to the promotion of co-operatives. It is clear that movements in these areas require substantial financial, technical and supervisory assistance from the state authorities if they are to survive or to gain a firm foothold in the first place. This support will have to continue until primary societies can achieve a degree of strength and efficiency, as well as a superstructure of secondary organisations, which will enable them to provide their own services and finance. At the same time it has been established that this dependence on government sometimes creates tensions and encourages attitudes contradictory to the co-operative principles of autonomy, initiative and self-help and the enlistment of the active interest and participation of members.

This confronts researchers with a challenge of the first order. All relevant experience and analysis will have to be examined and evaluated in an effort to find ways of providing emerging co-operatives with essential underpinning, while avoiding unnecessary intervention in their internal decision-making process and the kind of inefficiency that stems from the complacent assumption that the government will absorb losses. Limits will have to be defined and criteria, machinery and timetables developed for a gradual tapering-off of government support during the period of transition to autonomy and self-sufficiency. Specific research topics within this broad assignment might relate to the examination of the essential infrastructure for co-operatives which must be publicly provided, the relationship of co-operatives to state marketing boards, basic land reforms, co-operative legislation, the appropriate functions of co-operative commissioners, the influence on co-operative efficiency of monopoly concessions by the state, etc.

The Need for Detailed Local Surveys

It is clear, in respect of each of the above topics, that meaningful co-operative research in East Africa must be based on precise local information at the village level about a wide variety of economic, sociological and political factors. The process of gradually accumulating such data could be looked on as an objective in itself, in the secure knowledge that such local surveys would prove useful as background information for a large number of research projects over the years ahead. Moreover, the survey process itself may have an important educational influence in the village. Interviewing local people stimulates them to start thinking about their problems and discussing them among themselves, and this process could be formalised through a series of public seminars based on the surveys.

Yash Ghai

Co-operative Legislation in East Africa

While the official recognition of co-operatives in East Africa was granted in the 'forties, and legal provision enacted for their status and regulation, the current legislation on co-operatives in all three countries was passed only recently. Thus, the present Co-operative Societies Act in Kenya was enacted in 1966, in Tanzania in 1968 and in Uganda in 1970. The occasion for the replacement of the previous legislation and the introduction of the new Acts was in each case to reform the co-operative law and to provide for better control and regulation of societies. In this paper, I shall try to summarize in simple language the main provisions of the three Acts and to point to the differences between them, where these exist. Under each Act, the Minister responsible for the co-operatives (referred to henceforth as "the Minister") is authorized to make regulations to further implement the purposes and provisions of the Act; these regulations are equally binding on the co-operatives and some of their more important provisions will be discussed. It is as well to state that, in order to get a comprehensive picture of the legal provisions concerning co-operatives, reference should also be made to other laws, particularly on land tenure, rural credit and the marketing boards.

Formation, Registration, Dissolution, etc.

The Acts do not provide a clear and helpful definition of a co-operative society, other than to say that it is a society

---

Yash Ghai is a former Dean of the Faculty of Law, University of Dar-es-Salaam, and is currently a Visiting Research Professor at Yale University.

registered under the Act. However, a group or society can qualify for registration only if it has as its objects the promotion of the economic interests of its members in accordance with co-operative principles. There is no definition of either "the economic interests" or "co-operative principles". Some idea of the latter can be gathered from the various provisions of the Act, especially those dealing with the rights and obligations of the members and of the societies, as well as their rules or organization. As to the "economic interests", the reference points to the function of a society as a form of business or commercial organization, as an alternative, for example, to a company under the Companies Act. The "economic interests" are not restricted to any particular field, and the form of the co-operative societies can be used for different kinds of economic activities, especially producers' collectives, marketing arrangements, consumers' co-operatives, and credit societies, although the more specific provisions of the Acts are concerned more with the marketing co-operatives than others.

There is a kind of "hierarchy" of societies under the Acts, starting with the primary societies at the bottom and going up to the apex societies at the top. A primary society is defined in all three instances as a society in which membership is restricted to natural persons, i.e. individuals, but in Uganda and Tanzania it is clearly provided that a group of persons, for example, a company, may also become members if it has the written permission of the Registrar of Co-operatives. Although in Kenya the definition of a primary society seems to confine it to individuals, section 16 allows a group of persons to become a member of a "registered society" with the written permission of the Registrar. A "registered society" may, of course, be other than a primary society, and it is not obvious from the Act whether, for example, a company can be a member of a primary society.

The next layer is formed by what is called in Kenya and Uganda a co-operative union, and in Tanzania a secondary society. A co-operative union in the two former countries is defined as a registered society, the membership of which is confined to primary societies, while a Tanzanian secondary society is defined somewhat differently as a registered society which does not contain any members who are individuals. A Tanzanian secondary society may therefore be wider than a co-operative union in Kenya or Uganda and could include, for example, an apex society. It is perhaps for this reason that the Tanzanian Act has no separate definition of an apex society, which in Kenya and Uganda it is described as a registered society whose membership is restricted to co-operative unions and includes a society established to serve the co-operative movement by providing facilities for banking, insurance and the supply of goods or services. In Tanzania the existence of these "service organizations" as co-operative societies is recognized in section 4, dealing with societies which may be registered under the Act.

In addition to the above categories, Kenya has "district co-operative unions", in which membership is restricted to primary societies having their headquarters in the same district. Tanzania has the concept of a "national society", which means a registered society the area of whose operation extends throughout Tanganyika. There is nothing in the law to prevent the formation of equivalents of the Kenyan district co-operative unions and the Tanzanian national societies in the other countries. In practice, therefore, despite differences of terminology, the position in all the countries is similar.

In each country, a group of persons wishing to form a co-operative society must register it as such. Unless they have been granted registration, they cannot operate as a society. Whether an application for registration is granted or not depends on an offical, appointed in Tanzania by the President and in Kenya and Uganda by the Minister. In Tanzania and Uganda, the official is known as the Registrar of Co-operative Societies and in Kenya as the Commissioner for Co-operative Development (although in Uganda the Commissioner for Co-operative Development is *ex officio* Registrar); in this paper the designation of "Registrar" will be used throughout, even when the reference is to the Commissioner in Kenya. The Acts also provide for a Deputy Registrar and Assistant Registrars, but whereas in Tanzania the Deputy Registrar and the Assistant Registrars have the functions of the Registrar conferred on them by the Act itself, in the other two countries the Assistant

Registrars may perform these functions only in virtue of an order of the Minister. In addition to registration, these officials have various powers and responsibilities in relation to the co-operative movement, as we shall see.

An application has to be signed by at least 10 persons who are of the apparent age of 18 years or over and are resident within the area of operations of the proposed society or belong to the same occupation. The requirement of 10 signatures does not apply when one of the applicants is itself a registered society.

In such a case, the application has to be signed by an authorized official for each of the member societies, although in Kenya no more than 10 signatures are necessary. In Tanzania, the requirement that the applicant be of the same profession or that he reside in the same area applies only to societies whose object is the creation of funds to be lent to its members (a kind of "savings and credit society").

The application has to be accompanied by copies of the proposed by-laws of the society—three copies in Uganda and Tanzania, and four in Kenya. In Kenya and Uganda, the by-laws have to be in English, but in Tanzania no language is specified, so presumably they could be in Swahili. In addition, the Registrar may call for any other information that he may need. In all countries, the Registrar has the discretion whether to register the society or not. In Kenya and Uganda, no criteria for the exercise of the discretion are set out, except that, to be eligible, a society should be capable of promoting the economic interest of its members on the basis of co-operative principles. In Tanzania, the Registrar has to be satisfied of various matters, including adequate provisions for the proper financing and management of the society, before he can register the society. In particular, he must refuse to register if there is already in existence a society in the same locality or for the same purpose as in the application.

In Uganda, the Registrar needs the prior approval of the Minister before he can register an apex or union society. The Registrar may register a society even though not all the necessary conditions have been satisfied (in Uganda only if the non-compliance is not fundamental to the running of the society), if he feels that steps will be taken to fulfil them with due diligence by the sponsors. In such a case the society is registered as a probationary (Kenya and Tanzania) or provisional (Uganda) society. In Kenya, the maximum period for a "probationary" registration is 12 months and in Uganda 18 months, while no limit is prescribed in Tanzania. A probationary society has all the rights and obligations of a registered society, but it has to state clearly in its letterheads etc. that it is probationary. If the probationary society is duly registered, it ceases to be probationary; in Kenya and Tanzania, its registration dates back to the period of its initial registration as a probationary society. A probationary society may be cancelled at any time by the Registrar, and he need give no reason for cancellation.

A co-operative society may have either limited or unlimited liability, except that secondary societies (and in Tanzania, savings and credit societies also, except where the majority of the members are agriculturists) have to have limited liability. All societies with limited liability have to carry the word "Limited" as the last word in their names.

The by-laws of the society, which are binding on its members, can be changed by the society, but such changes need the approval of the Registrar. In addition, the Registrar can require a society to amend its by-laws, and in case of default, he can proceed to amend them himself. Before the registration of a society, the Registrar can direct it to amend the proposed by-laws as a condition of registration.

Amalgamation, Division and Dissolution

Once a society has been registered, it may decide that it wants to join with a neighbouring society or it may find that it is too large or covers too large an area of operations and that better results might be achieved if it were to split into two or more societies. Under the law, amalgamations and divisions are not always the result of the free and voluntary decision of the society; it is possible for the government to order amalgamations and divisions. Both in amalgamation or division, the original society or societies is dissolved. The need therefore arises to protect the interests of the members and creditors of the original society or societies, and certain safeguards and special procedures have been established for amalgamating or dividing societies. The power of the government to order amalgamation or division is also a source of potentially serious intervention in the affairs of a society. The laws of the three countries show significant differences in this area, which can be related to the differences in their policies as regards co-operatives. In Tanzania those processes are easiest, and the interests of the minority (or opposing members) as well as of creditors are more clearly subordinated to those of the co-operative movement than in the other two countries. The government's powers of intervention are greater in Tanzania than elsewhere, and greater in Uganda than in Kenya.

As regards voluntary amalgamation, the first step is to obtain the approval of the Registrar. No criteria are laid down for the guidance of the Registrar in deciding whether or not to withhold his approval. In Uganda and Tanzania, the procedure thereafter is relatively simple: the societies concerned have to convene a meeting of their members for which "reasonable notice" (Tanzania) or 15 days' notice (Uganda) has been given. The meeting's resolution in favour of amalgamation is valid only if at least three-quarters (Uganda) or two-thirds (Tanzania) of the members present vote for it. In Uganda, the affirmative resolutions are by themselves enough to effect the transfer of the assets and liabilities of the old societies to the new one, but in Tanzania, an order of the Registrar is necessary to transfer the assets, as well as to cancel the registration of the old societies and to provide for that of the amalgamation and its by-laws. The Uganda legislation is silent as to the procedure for the registration of the new society and its by-laws, as well as the cancellation of the old ones; no doubt the regulations to be enacted thereunder will take care of this point. Neither in Uganda nor in Tanzania is there any special provision for those members who are opposed to the amalgamation. In Uganda, a creditor of either society can oppose the proposal for amalgamation by giving written notice, upon which the amalgamation cannot take place until he has been satisfied or an agreement has been reached for payment to be made to him. In case of dispute, the creditor can appeal to the Registrar within 90 days, and the Registrar's decision is final. Unfortunately, the drafting of the Uganda legislation is rather careless, and a number of problems may arise in practice. First, there is no provision for notice to be given to a creditor that an amalgamation is proposed, so that he can lodge his objection. Second, a creditor has to give notice one month before the date fixed for the amalgamation, whereas 15 days' notice is all that is required for a meeting at which the decision on the amalgamation can be made, and there is no rule which requires that the active date of amalgamation be fixed sufficiently far in advance so that a creditor has a chance to give the necessary notice. Third, there is a provision, as we have already seen, whereby the affirmative resolutions of the societies have the effect *ipso facto* of transferring their assets and liabilities to the new society, so that it is not clear what the effect of a creditor's notice is. Fourth, it is not clear what is meant by the "appeal" that a creditor can make to the Registrar. Apart from the fact that the word "appeal" seems a strange one to use in this context, it is not obvious what the powers of the Registrar are. Can he force the society to make a payment which he deems reasonable? If so, which society?

The Tanzania rules overcome some of these problems. Amalgamation is affected by an order of the Registrar, which has to be published in the *Gazette*; the order specifies the date of the amalgamation, dissolves the old society and registers the new, and transfers the assets to the new society. The Registrar may refuse to make the order if he is not satisfied that the amalgamation is not against the interest of the members or against the public interest; and in his order he can issue the directions necessary for safeguarding the interests of any person. Presumably this power could be used to protect creditors, although there seems to be no provision whereby a creditor has to be informed of the proposed amalgamation or can make representations to the Registrar.

The Kenya provisions are the most thorough-going. The societies intending to merge need to have the prior approval of the Registrar. Each has to pass a special resolution (i.e. a resolution passed by a majority of three-quarters of the members present and voting at a special general meeting), called the preliminary resolution, in favour of amalgamation. A copy of the resolution has to be sent to all the members, the creditors, and "all other persons whose interests in any of the societies will be affected by the amalgamation". Any of these groups of persons may demand from the society the satisfaction of his claims before the amalgamation is effected, which in the case of a member will mean the return of his share capital. After these notices have been received, each of the societies holds another special general meeting, at which the demands are considered, and if the societies still want to proceed to amalgamation, they have to make provision by resolution ("secondary resolution") for the satisfaction of the claims (in the case of the third category of claimants, for such claimants and in such manner as the Registrar may determine). These resolutions become effective when the society confirms the preliminary resolution, by a two-thirds majority of those present and voting. The active amalgamation takes place when the Registrar registers the new society and its by-laws, on being satisfied that the provisions of the secondary resolutions have been complied with. The registration has the effect *ipso facto* of cancelling the registration of the old societies, of vesting all their assets in the new one, and of transferring the membership in the old societies to the new. Persons with claims against any of the old societies which have not been dealt with by a secondary resolution may pursue their claims against the new society.

Amalgamation can also be forced upon societies by the government, but here again there are differences between the three countries. In Tanzania, the Registrar may require societies to amalgamate if he thinks it is in their interests to amalgamate (and amalgamation is not against the public interest). Thereupon the societies have to prepare by-laws for the amalgamated society within a specified period, on the approval of which the Registrar registers the new society and may make any order about assets, etc. that he is authorized to make in the case of a voluntary merger. If a society fails to obey his orders to amalgamate with another society or societies, he may cancel its registration.

In Uganda, the decision as regards compulsory amalgamation is made by the Minister; if he is satisfied that it is in the public interest or in the interest of the co-operative movement or it is for the purpose of ensuring the proper management of any society, he may by a notice in the *Gazette* direct that any two or more societies shall amalgamate. He may appoint an auditor, who, after consultation with the societies, if he so wishes, advises the Minister on the form and procedure of amalgamation, although it is not clear what precisely his powers and functions are, nor is it clear what the purpose of the mandatory special general meetings of the societies is. Creditors and other interested persons have to be informed by the societies of the order for amalgamation and may then submit their claims (within 30 days of the *Gazette* notice). If a society fails to reach an agreement with them, the matter is referred to the Minister for a final ruling. Any society (or its officer) which refuses to carry out the Minister's orders is guilty of a criminal offence and is liable to a fine. It is, however, not clear when the active amalgamation takes place, nor is it obvious whether the societies have any power to disregard any of the instructions of the Minister. In Kenya, the Registrar issues the order to amalgamate, but there is a right of appeal to the Minister. Here again it is not obvious what the effect of the Registrar's order is and the law says that the order shall have the effect of a preliminary resolution. Does it mean that the members of the societies can reject the secondary or final resolution, and thus frustrate the order, or does it merely mean that the order dispenses with the need for a preliminary resolution? Nor is it clear what the procedure for amalgamation is; is it the same as for a voluntary merger, with the exception of the preliminary resolution?

Division

A division of a society is in some respects the opposite of an amalgamation; it is a process whereby a society is split into two or more societies. Like amalgamation, division can either be voluntary or compulsory, except that in Kenya there cannot be a compulsory division. The procedure for voluntary division is approximately the same in all three countries; the society has to approve the resolution for division by a special majority (three-quarters in Kenya and Uganda, two-thirds in Tanzania). The resolution has to set out the terms of the proposed division, i.e. the division of the assets and liabilities among the new societies, the areas of their operations, and their membership. In Tanzania, there is no need for further action on the part of the society; the Registrar may by a *Gazette* notice divide the society into new societies if he is satisfied that the division is not against the interests of the members or the public. His order specifies the date of division, the names of the new societies and the manner in which the assets and liabilities are to be divided. Presumably his order will be in the same terms as the resolution of the society in these respects, but this is not expressly provided for. As in the case of amalgamation, there are no safeguards to protect the interests of the creditors and others, but the Registrar may give such directions as he considers necessary for this purpose.

In Kenya and Uganda, the society has to inform members and creditors of the preliminary resolution and to give them the opportunity to submit claims; the subsequent procedure for claims, secondary resolutions, final resolution and the Registrar's approval is similar to that for amalgamation.

In the case of a compulsory division in Tanzania, the Registrar issues a notice requiring a society to divide itself, if he is satisfied that it is in its interest to do so and is not against the public interest. The notice may specify the manner in which assets and liabilities are to be divided, and other matters which need to be provided for in a resolution on voluntary division. The society has to prepare by-laws for the new societies, upon approval of which the Registrar registers the new societies, thereby automatically dissolving the old one. In Uganda, the procedure for compulsory division is identical, *mutatis mutandis,* with that for compulsory amalgamation, with similar ambiguities and uncertainties.

Dissolution

In a sense, both amalgamation and division are means whereby a society ceases to exist as such, but the intention is not to bring the operations to an end but to provide for their management on a smaller or larger scale. The dissolution proper of a society takes place when its corporate character is completely terminated and its operations cease. A society may be dissolved either by a voluntary decision of its members or compulsorily by an order of cancellation by the Registrar. However, even in the former case, the permission of the Registrar is necessary, since in no instance can a society be dissolved or wound up without his order. In a voluntary dissolution, there has to be an application to him, supported by three-quarters of all the members. Compulsory cancellation can be made on a number of different grounds. The Registrar may order cancellation of registration after receiving the report of an enquiry into the affairs or an inspection of the books of the society (as to when the enquiry or inspection may take place, see below). He may also cancel registration when the number of members fall below the statutory minimum, i.e. 10 in the case of primary societies. In Tanzania, there are additional grounds for dissolution; societies which disregard instructions to merge or divide may have their registrations cancelled, as well as societies which the Registrar has reasonable cause to believe have not commenced or have ceased to carry on business (three months after the date of a notice in the *Gazette*). Finally, the Registrar may, after due enquiry, cancel the registration of any society, which, having been a member of a secondary society, has been expelled or has withdrawn from membership of that secondary society. Appeals to the Minister by any member of a society whose registration has been cancelled are provided for, in Tanzania within one month and in the other countries within two months.

When a society's registration is cancelled, the Registrar may appoint a liquidator or liquidators (as in Kenya and Uganda), in whom are vested all the assets of the society and whose function it is to wind up the society and its affairs. The laws provide in detail as to the order of priority of the claims on its assets, as well as to the powers and duties of the liquidator. When the assets fall short of the liabilities, the general principles of the law of bankruptcy apply. It is not proposed in this paper to examine the provision for the liquidation of societies, since the rules are specialized and technical.

Benefits and Liabilities of Registration as a Co-operative

A co-operative society differs from an unincorporated group of farmers in various ways, which constitute the benefits of registration. In pursuance of the policy of development through co-operative enterprise, the law confers special privileges on co-operative societies, privileges which are not available to unregistered groups. In return for these benefits, certain duties and obligations are imposed on them, as well as a high degree of control over their activities by the government. I turn first to the benefits.

By virtue of registration, a society becomes a body corporate. This means that it acquires a legal personality of its own, distinct and separate from that of its members. A society has a perpetual succession, i.e. its existence is not affected by the death of one or more members. In instances when the society has a limited liability, its members are not liable for the debts and obligations of the society beyond the amount of unpaid shares and other dues owing to the society. In an unlimited society, the members are responsible for its liabilities. In that sense, a limited-liability society can be compared to a company under the Companies Act, and an unlimited society to a partnership. The society can enter into transactions, creating rights and liabilities, on its own or through the agency of its officials. It can acquire, hold and dispose of movable or immovable property (i.e. personal property or real estate) of any kind, enter into contracts, institute and defend suits and other legal proceedings, and do all such things as are necessary for the purpose of its constitution.

In addition to the above advantages, which are common to various other incorporated groups, a co-operative society has other advantages which are peculiar to itself. The society has prior claims on the crops, produce, cattle, implements, raw materials and manufactured goods of its members in relation to the loans (whether cash or in kind, for example, seeds and fertilizer) it has advanced to them, save only for the superior claims of the government or of the landlord for rent. In other words, if a member's liabilities exceed his assets, and various creditors are seeking to get at his assets, the society is given a preference over all other creditors with the above-mentioned exceptions. This privilege of the society extends to a person who has ceased to be a member for a period of two years from the date when the loan was supplied to him. In addition, the society has a claim on the assets of a member which are in its hands, for example, shares, dividends, etc., and may retain all or part of these for itself to the amount owed to it by the member or a past member, as payment towards such debts. On the other hand, the share of a member is privileged against attachment or sale by order of court at the instance of other creditors, including official receivers in bankruptcies.

The society has other privileges in relation to its members. The liability of a past member for the debts of the society at the time he ceased to be a member continues for two years thereafter, while the estate of a deceased member is similarly liable for a year after death. When a member dies, the society can either transfer his interests or shares to his nominee or (if there is none) to his personal representative or pay him a sum equal to the value of the interests or shares, except that, if the society has unlimited liability, the nominee or representative can claim payment in lieu of shares and, in the case of limited-liability societies, shares have to be transferred, but if he is not qualified to become a member, he has to nominate, within one month, a person to whom the shares can be transferred.

In Tanzania and Uganda (but apparently not in Kenya), the President and the Minister of Finance, respectively, have the power to exempt from taxation the accumulated funds of the society or the income from it received by the members, and to waive stamp duties otherwise payable on the documents of the societies, as well as registration fees.

The most significant powers of the societies are those in relation to the marketing of produce. Societies which have as one of their objects the disposal of agricultural produce (in Tanzania only, also "handicrafts or mining") may bind their members, either in the by-laws or by a separate contractual document, to sell all or a specified amount of their produce to or through the society. The society may provide for liquidated damages (i.e. fixed amounts per unit of weight or other measure) for breach of this obligation to sell to it. The society acquires by means of such a contract a claim on the produce of the members, whether it actually exists or is being produced, and the obligation to sell to the society runs with the land, etc., which means that, if the member sells or transfers his land to someone else, the new occupier is bound in the same way as the member. In Kenya, the society can enforce its claim only if it has registered the contract; Tanzania and Uganda are silent on the point of registration. The society also has a claim upon the sale of the produce stipulated in the contract. In Kenya, the society is permitted to pledge the produce the members are under an obligation to sell as security for loans made to the society, provided that a resolution to that effect is passed at the general meeting. Any person who knowingly induces a member to break his contract to sell through the society is guilty of an offence.

In certain instances, the society may be given powers of marketing produce other than that of its own members. This is possible only in Kenya and Tanzania. The principle is that, if a society handles the bulk of the produce of a specified kind, it may seek a monopoly of the marketing of that produce, so that even non-members have to sell to or through the society. The monopoly may relate either to the entire country, if the society operates on a nation-wide basis, or to the part of the country covered by its operations. Tanzania has more stringent provisions for the grant of monopoly than Kenya. In the latter country, if a society which handles at least 60% of a particular kind of produce in the whole or a part of the country, as the case may be, applies to the Minister, he may make the necessary order for sale to or through the co-operative. In Tanzania, the society may make an application only if it is approved by a resolution at a general meeting at which two-thirds of the members are present, and the members not only are responsible for 75% of the produce, but their number also constitutes at least 75% of all the producers. The application is made to the Registrar, who will make the order only if it is in the general interest of the relevant industry. He has to publish his intention to make the order in the *Gazette,* and to give an opportunity to objectors to present their case. In Tanzania, but not in Kenya, an existing contract for sale elsewhere is not invalidated, so long as it was made before the resolution of the society seeking the monopoly, but the exemption from invalidation expires a year after the society has given the directions for compulsory sale. The Minister has the power to vary or cancel the order on appeal. Again, in Tanzania, but not in Kenya, there are provisions for the revocation of the order; the Registrar may do so, if its continuance is not in the interests of the industry, if less than two-thirds of the affected producers are members, if in the preceding year they produced less than two-thirds of the total produce, and if more than a third of the members vote for revocation. He has to cancel the order if 75% of the primary societies affected by the order vote in favour of revocation.

Non-members are bound by all the conditions and obligations as if they were members. In Tanzania, they are, however, exempt from the obligation to pay any membership fee or share subscription; in Kenya, the society may make deductions from the sums owed to it as payments towards the purchase of shares. In both countries, such non-members have a right to become members upon the payment of the necessary fees etc.; in Kenya, the non-member can require the society to make deductions for payments due to him until the subscription has been completely paid.

The lawful functioning of some of the above privileges requires that the co-operative societies are exempt from certain legal rules. The most important of these are in the area of the law of contract. Normally, an agreement which compels one to dispose of one's services or products in a particular way or restricts their disposal in some way runs the risk of being void and of no legal effect; if the restrictions are unreasonable, the law disregards the agreement, as being against public policy. The agreement whereby a society binds its members to sell only to itself might well be declared unlawful, but the Acts state clearly that no such contracts are to be void as being in restraint of trade. Secondly, it is not normally possible to sell something which does not exist at the time the contract was formed, for example, a future crop. Again, a society's contract in relation to such future products is expressly provided for in the Acts. Thirdly, in some instances, persons under the age of 21 years, i.e. under the age of majority, cannot enter into certain types of contract. Normally, a contract to join a co-operative and to be bound by its rules would not be regarded as binding on such a member, but the Acts provide that, when a person who has attained the age of 18 years (the minimum age for membership) but not that of majority becomes a member, he shall, for the purpose of contracting with the society, be taken to be of full age.

The Management of Co-operative Societies

I shall examine the provisions for the management of a society before turning to those for control, and the duties and obligations of the society. The principles of management are basic to the co-operative movement, and distinguish it from other forms of business organization.

Co-operatives are planned to be run on democratic lines, so that the basic decisions about their organization and operation are made by the members themselves. However, as we have already seen, the law lays down certain rules for their establishment and operation which restrict the freedom of the members to take certain forms of decision, and we shall see later that the Registrar has powers to give binding directions to the co-operatives on several matters of organization and operation. Thus, while the ideal is far from realized, in so far as decisions are left to the co-operatives, all the members are deemed to have equal rights. Each member has one vote, regardless of the number of shares he may hold.

Apart from the provisions in the Acts and the regulations made thereunder, a co-operative has to function according to its by-laws, which may be regarded as its constitution. The by-laws are binding on the members, and set out their rights and obligations *vis-à-vis* the society, and among themselves. They can and generally do provide for the imposition of fines on members who are in breach of their obligations.

The Ugandan and Kenyan Acts have relatively little to say on the management of a society, but the Kenyan regulations contain some provisions on this. The position in all three countries, however, is similar. The supreme authority of the society is vested in the general meeting of members. The general meeting has to take place once a year, but provisions exist for calling it into session (as a special general meeting) more often, if necessary for the disposal of business or if directed by the Registrar. Decisions are made by majority vote, except in certain specified instances, when a higher vote is necessary, as, for example, in the case of amalgamation. As the general meeting takes place only a few times a year, much of the day-to-day management of the society is left to an elected committee, known as the "management committee". The committee has all the powers necessary for the performance of its duties, including powers to borrow. The committee is empowered to appoint a manager and other persons necessary to assist him in the discharge of his duties; the approval of the Registrar is necessary before these appointments can be made. In addition, the Registrar may direct the committee to dismiss any of the persons so employed, if he finds the discharge of his duties unsatisfactory.

The Registrar has further powers in relation to the committee. If, in his opinion, the conduct of the committee is unsatisfactory, he may, after considering the objections of the committee thereto, in a general meeting dissolve the committee, direct the society to elect a new committee or himself appoint two or more persons to sit as the committee, with the powers thereof, initially for two years but with an option to extend it for a maximum of another two years. In Tanzania, if the society receives financial assistance from the government, the Registrar may appoint special members to the committee, up to one-third of the ordinary members, if he thinks it desirable to do so in the interests of the public or the society.

There is the general principle that no committee member should hold an office in the society which carries a salary or other remuneration. In Uganda, there is no rule about the honorarium to be paid to committee members; in Kenya, an honorarium or remuneration is permitted if the Commissioner is consulted and the general meeting approves. In Tanzania, committee members may receive an honorarium (up to 500 shillings per annum for a primary, and 2000 shillings for a secondary society) if (*a*) it has been authorized by a resolution of the general meeting, and (*b*) the Registrar has given his approval. The total sum paid by any society to its committee members by way of honoraria is not to exceed 50% of its annual net surplus.

The societies and their committees have to operate in accordance with the principles and rules laid down in the Acts or the regulations made thereunder. Some of these principles and rules have been discussed already, and some others will be examined now. They can be divided into two kinds: rules laying down the principles of operation of a society, and rules dealing with the control and supervision by the government of the affairs of the society. The distinction is not a clear one, for the effect of many rules in the first category in fact depends upon the discretion of government officials, but it is made here, as it helps in the elucidation of the law. In the first category, the most important provisions are those which deal with the finances of the society. The society has to prepare annual accounts of the financial transactions and position (in Kenya, the Registrar can require the society to appoint an accountant, to be paid by the society, for the purpose). The Registrar has to have the accounts audited by an auditor appointed by himself or (in Kenya and Uganda) an auditor nominated by the society and approved by him. The auditor has to be given access to all the books and records of the society, and can summon any member or agent of the society to supply information in regard to the transactions or management of the society. The accounts have to be approved by the general meeting of the society before submission to the Registrar for his approval. In Uganda and Tanzania, the society has also to present to the Minister (Uganda) and the Registrar

(Tanzania) estimates of income and expenditure for the following year, which on his approval become the basis and authority for the expenditure of the society's funds. No money can be spent unless his approval has been obtained, and he has the power to substitute his own estimates for those proposed by the society.

There are clear and strict rules on the powers of a society to borrow or lend money, and on the manner of the disposal of its funds. As a rule, a society cannot lend money or give credit to any person other than a member, but, if the Registrar gives his permission, the society may make loans to another registered society, and with similar permission in Kenya and Uganda, it may stand surety for an employee, where the loan is for the benefit of the society, for example, to enable the manager to buy a car for the more efficient execution of his duties. In Tanzania, if the Registrar consents, a loan may be made to any person if it is for an agricultural purpose. When the main object or one of the objects of a society is to supply commodities to the members, it cannot make loans or give credit without the permission of the Registrar, who can impose limits and conditions thereon. The Registrar (the Minister in Uganda) can prohibit or restrict the lending of money on the security of immoveable property, i.e. land and permanent buildings, presumably in order to ensure that the loans are small and short-term, while in Tanzania a society with unlimited liability cannot make loans on the security of a moveable property without the Registrar's permission. In Tanzania, a marketing society may make loans only up to 75% of the estimated value of the products expected to be delivered to it for marketing.

A society cannot borrow from a non-member, except in accordance with the rules laid down by the Minister or in the by-laws. Hire-purchase agreements are deemed to constitute loans to the society and so are covered by the above restriction. The Minister's interest is to ensure that the society does not indulge in excessive borrowing and that the terms of the loans are not too disadvantageous to the society. Quite apart from borrowing from or lending to non-members, the society can enter into any transactions with non-members to the extent of and subject to the terms and conditions laid down by the Minister. In Kenya, the total value of transactions with non-members in any particular produce should not exceed one-half of all the transactions in a year in that produce, and the profits made from such transactions are to be deposited in a reserve fund and are not available for distribution to the members, except when the Minister has made an order for compulsory marketing through the society. The reasons for the policy of restrictions on transactions with non-members would appear to be twofold: to protect the society against injudicious and disadvantageous contracts, and to preserve the co-operative basis of the society, which consists in relations and transactions between the members themselves.

To turn to the restrictions on the disposal of funds. A society can invest or deposit its funds only in specified securities or financial institutions, being limited to banks (including the Post Office Savings Bank) or other registered societies (in Kenya and Uganda) or registered companies (in Uganda) approved by the Registrar (Kenya) or the Minister (Uganda). In addition, in all three countries, the Registrar or the Minister may authorize other forms of investments or deposits.

The payments a society makes to its members are of two kinds—dividends and bonus. Dividends are based on the proportion of the shares of the members, i.e. on their capital investment in the society, while the bonus is based on the proportion of the member's puchases from the society or his participation in such business, for example, the delivery and sale of produce to the society. In keeping with co-operative principles, the member's services rather than his capital contribution are regarded as important, and it would be contrary to those principles that the activities of a co-operative society should provide a high return on capital. The law thus restricts the rate of dividends; in Kenya and Uganda, the maximum permitted rate is 10%, while in Tanzania it is 5%.

Dividends or bonuses can be paid only in circumstances in which, in any financial year, the society's operations result in a surplus, i.e. its profits exceed its operating costs and liabilities. The wording in Kenya seems to suggest that in such a situation the society has to declare a bonus, while in the other two countries the matter is left to the option of the society. In Kenya, the bonus has to be declared, although it may not be actually distributed, if needed for further investment, in which case the members have to be issued with bonus certificates, redeemable in the future from a revolving fund. In all three countries, any proposals to declare dividends or bonuses have to be approved by the general meeting. The permission of the Registrar is also necessary, along with his written acknowledgment that a balance sheet disclosing the surplus funds has been lodged with him. A society with unlimited liability which advances money or goods to any member in excess of the money or the value of the goods deposited by him cannot pay a dividend for a period of 10 years from the date of its registration; this is presumably to ensure that the society's financial position is strengthened and there is less occasion to call on the members to contribute to meet the liabilities of the society.

Before any money becomes payable as bonus or dividend, the society has to provide for certain compulsory contributions or savings. In all three countries, a society which does or can derive a surplus from its transactions has to maintain a reserve fund. In the case of societies with unlimited liability, the amount transferred to the reserve fund has to be at least 25% of the surplus, while in other instances the proportion is as laid down in the rules or by-laws (it is currently 25% in Kenya and 20% in Tanzania). The reserve fund is intended to build up the financial strength of the society or to be used for its capital expenditure. The fund is indivisible and individual members have no claim on it—a rule which seeks to ensure that the reserve funds are not dissipated as profits distributed to the members. Secondly, the societies have to contribute to an Audit and Supervision Fund, which is held and administered by the Registrar, except when the functions of audit and supervision are delegated to a society. The amount of the contribution is determined by the Registrar. In Uganda, there is a further compulsory contribution; each society has to contribute up to 1% of its surplus (the actual percentage is determined by the Minister) to a National Co-operative Education Fund, a fund which is controlled by the

Minister, who has to use it for furthering co-operative education among members, officers and any other employees of the society.

Implicit in the operating principles discussed above is the nature and degree of governmental control over the activities of the co-operative movement. We have thus seen that the Registrar or the Minister can refuse to register a society, compulsorily amend its by-laws, dissolve the committee and set up his own supervisors and managers, order compulsory amalgamation or division (except in Kenya), dismiss the employees of a society, cancel the registration of a society and make rules for the conduct of societies. A further series of controls is available through the financial provisions. Finally, I shall look at some further powers of control vested in the government. The Registrar, either on his own initiative or at the request of the majority of the committee or not less than one-third of the members, may cause an enquiry to be made into the constitution, activities and financial affairs of a society. He can also order an inspection of the books of the society, if requested by a creditor of the society, as long as the sum owing to the creditor has become due and payment has not been made to him despite demand. The effects of an inquiry or inspection in relation to the Registrar's powers to dissolve the society have already been noticed. In addition, the results of the inquiry or inspection may provide the basis of a surcharge which the Registrar can levy upon a member or officer, past or present, if it is revealed that he has made or authorized an unlawful payment or has by negligence or misconduct caused a deficiency or a loss or a failure to take into account or caused damage to property of the society. The surcharge may, in the discretion of the Registrar, equal the amount of the loss or such lesser sum as he thinks reasonable in the circumstances of the case. If the surcharge is under 2 000 shillings, an appeal lies to the Minister; if over, the appeal is to the High Court.

Conclusion

The purpose of this paper has been to describe the provisions of the co-operative legislation in East Africa. No comments have been made on the reasonableness, feasibility or practicability of the provisions, nor has an evaluation been made of how far they have been implemented in practice. A previous conference at the Scandinavian Institute of African Studies dealt with many of these issues (the proceedings were reported in *Co-operatives and Rural Development in East Africa,* edited by Carl Gösta Widstrand). One comment may, however, be made in conclusion now. The general principles of the co-operative movement emphasize the democracy, autonomy, initiative and self-reliance of the members. In East Africa, these principles are seriously compromised by the overwhelming powers vested in the government, so that sometimes the movement is co-operative in little else than name. Perhaps at the present stage in East Africa, this dilemma is inevitable. The co-operative movement there has not generally been spontaneous but has often been imposed from above, because the government, for a variety of reasons, including predominantly the desire to keep out non-African middlemen, has perceived the desirability of the co-operative form as a means of development. Given the general illiteracy and the farmers' ignorance of co-operative principles and the expertise necessary to make them operative, the government has felt it necessary to intervene at all levels of the movement to ensure its viability. The co-operative movement has invariably been presented as an instrument of socialism. The legislation indicates that this is not necessarily so. The discussions within Tanzania on the applicability of the co-operative laws to *Ujamaa* villages have highlighted this fact. The legislation needs to be much more explicitly communalistically based if it is to promote the purposes of socialism.

Pheroze Nowrojee

The Settlement of Disputes in Co-operative Societies

The steep rise in the numbers and significance of co-operative societies in the East African countries in the last decade has been reflected in the increased appearance in the courts of law of problems arising out of the law on co-operatives. Such cases are of importance alike to co-operators, government officials, lawyers and courts. A number of recent decisions have dealt with and clarified important points of law in respect of the settlement of disputes in co-operative societies. Special regard has been paid in these decisions to the question of the ouster of the jurisdiction of the courts, for the legislation affecting co-operatives envisages the exclusion of the courts in the settlement of disputes within the co-operative movement, and provides specific alternative methods. This paper therefore seeks

(*a*) First, to establish what constitutes a dispute under co-operative law;

(*b*) Then, to examine what happens when a dispute comes into existence; and

(*c*) Finally, to evaluate the methods of settlement.

The provisions regarding the settlement of disputes are to be found in the principal act, the Co-operative Societies Act, in each of the three countries, in the rules made thereunder, and in the by-laws of each society.

The Legislation

Section 73 (1) and (2) of the Co-operative Societies Act of Uganda[1] (Act No. 30 of 1970) reads as follows:

Pherozee Nowrojee, who graduated from the University of Dares-Salaam, is a practising lawyer in Nairobi.

73. (1) If any dispute touching the business of a registered society arises,

(*a*) among the members, past members and persons claiming through members, past members and deceased members; or

(*b*) between a member, past member or person claiming through a member, past member or deceased member, and the society, its committee or any officer or past officer of the society; or

(*c*) between the society or its committee and any officer or past officer of the society; or

(*d*) between the society and any other registered society, such dispute shall be referred to the Registrar for decision.

(2) A claim by a registered society for any debt or demand due to it from a member, past member or the nominee, heir or legal representative of a deceased member, whether such debt or demand be admitted or not, shall be deemed to be a dispute within the meaning of subsection (1) of this section.

What is a Dispute?

The word "dispute" has not been defined in any of the three acts. It is therefore not a technical term carrying a fixed or special meaning in law. It is accordingly to be given its ordinary and natural meaning: "Thus it would mean no more than 'a controversy' or 'a quarrel'."[2] The word "dispute" includes all matters which could form the subject of civil litigation[3] but is also, of course, wider than that. Likewise "disputes" are not confined to matters involving only financial loss, though these are the most prevalent. They would include any matter giving rise to some legal loss or liability.[4] Election disputes would be examples of the latter which need not give rise to any financial loss but which would nonetheless be disputes under the Acts.

Because, before the arbitration provisions come into operation, it may be necessary for the Registrar of Co-operative Societies (in Kenya, the Commissioner for Co-operative Development) to satisfy himself that a dispute exists, we must consider some objections that have been raised in the courts against certain disputes being held to be disputes under the acts. If such objections are successful, the effect is to have the dispute adjudicated upon by the courts. If not, then the dispute falls to be decided under the arbitration provisions of the Acts. Firstly, it has been objected that, if a party admits the facts of a claim against him (though not the claim), there can be no dispute. The courts have rejected this and held that such admission of facts must be distinguished from an admission of liability thereon.[5] But they have been willing to go even further. Even an admission of the claim itself does not, of itself, prevent the matter being a dispute under the Acts. Nor does mere willingness to pay the claim at different times prevent a dispute from arising. A "dispute" comes into existence when the claim is not met upon demand, whether because of refusal, neglect or inability to pay then or to satisfy the legal demand.[6] Thus the courts have rejected the second objection.

But, in doing so, they have had to consider the purpose and effect of one of the more unclear provisions of the law. It will have been noted that sub-section (2) of the relevant provisions of the Uganda and Kenya Acts (quoted earlier) deals also with the admission by members of the claims of the society. The sub-section provides that, notwithstanding such admission, a dispute arises. It had been argued, and held, in the case of *Republic v. Commissioner for Co-operative Development ex p. Kibuthi* (1969) E.A. 168, that these provisions implied that in the converse case, that is, where it was the *society* which was admitting its member's claim, the admission prevented the matter from being a dispute under sub-section (1) and the Act. This finding was upset in the later case of *Gatanga Coffee Growers Co-operative Society Limited v. Gitau* (1970) E.A. 361, which made it clear that the main, if not the sole purpose of the sub-section was the removal of any doubts which might be thought to exist that claims by a society which were admitted by a member were not disputes within the Act. The rationale, it is submitted, is to prevent the society, which is always expected to be financially stronger than the individual member, from involving the latter in long and expensive litigation.

The courts have also rejected the third objection: that if there is no defence, in fact or in law, to the claim, then there is no dispute. The courts have been clear that the validity or otherwise of the defence to a claim is not material to the question whether or not a dispute exists.[7] To hold otherwise in such situations would confuse the existence of a dispute with the merits of that dispute. Equally untenable is the view that, because the claim itself is a bad one or even a false one, there is no dispute. So long as a claim is asserted by one party and denied by the other, be the claim a false one or a true one, or whether it ultimately turns out to be false or true, there is a dispute.[8]

Thus, co-operative officers in the field will find that the problems that arise in societies within their jurisdiction will almost invariably constitute such disputes as have been discussed above. But that does not conclude the matter there. For before such dispute can be referred to the Registrar for arbitration, and the jurisdiction of the courts excluded, three other requirements must be satisfied:

(*a*) The dispute must be one "concerning the business of the society".

(*b*) The dispute must be between the parties prescribed by the Acts.

(*c*) The dispute must be between these prescribed parties in their capacity as such.

"Concerning the Business of the Society"

This requirement is laid down by the Acts themselves and, like the word "dispute", the term "concerning" or "touching" the business of the society has not been defined. Though it limits the opening words "any dispute", the term itself has wide application. The words "concerning" or "touching" were clearly not intended to restrict the meaning of the word "business". They were designed to enlarge its scope. The disputes were not to be restricted to matters arising from and out of the business of the society but were also extended to matters which in some way concerned or related to the business of the society.[9]

In the *Gatanga* case the court held that "The expression 'business of the society', in my opinion, covers every activity of the society within the orbit of its by-laws and rules." Again, the interpretation given is wide and the legislation held to cover as broad an area of dispute as is possible within the subsequent provisos, that is, as broad as is relevant to the area of co-operative transactions. In determining that area, the by-laws are obviously relevant. They lay down the powers of the management committee of a society, the rights and duties of members, and directions as to the society's financial transactions, the conduct of business at meetings and elections and the admission and expulsion of members. These are all fruitful sources of disputes between the various prescribed parties. The objects of a society are also contained in the by-laws. But it must be remembered that the business of a society is wider than only the matters found in the objects, and includes all the transactions necessary to the achievement of those objects, the working of the society and the attainment of co-operative goals.

The Prescribed Parties

The Acts (in Tanzania the Rules) lay down that the disputes which they consider should be referred to the Registrar and excluded from the courts must be disputes between certain parties only. They specify those parties. They consist of members, past members, persons claiming through them and deceased members, the society, its committee, its officers, and other registered societies. The prescribed parties assisted by the section are therefore co-operators and co-operators only. This is further underscored by the fact that a dispute relating to transactions arising out of the co-operative movement is covered by the section, even though the parties thereto are no longer co-operators. Such disputes involving past members or past officers or persons claiming through past or deceased or current members must, however, have arisen while such party was a member of the society or by reference to the period during which he was or is a member. Thus, should a past member subsequently enter into an agreement with the society, any dispute arising out of that agreement would not be referred to the Registrar, notwithstanding that it may be a dispute concerning the business of the society and is apparently between two of the prescribed parties. Other difficulties, too, present themselves in relation to past members. What societies must guard against is seeking, under these provisions, to obtain enforcement through the arbitration machinery of any authority over parties who have ceased to be members but still remain within the area of the society's operations.[10]

Most of the disputes reaching the courts have been between members, on the one hand, and the society, on the other. This has only reflected the current difficulties in the co-operative movements, arising out of non-responsive management, poor staffing, and problems of organisation and financial control.[11] But it will be noted from a perusal of the whole subsection that in Kenya another very common group of disputes is missing therefrom. Disputes between the society, on the one hand, and its officers, on the other, are *not* covered. This is a frequent and recognised head of dispute and its omission in the current act is illogical. Past Kenyan legislation did include such disputes. An explanation of its omission in the new Act may lie in the complementary change in the definition of "officer". "Officer" is now meant to include an employee of the society. Though, as is shown hereunder, a dispute with an employee is not, and should not, be protected by the section (as it appears to be under the Uganda Act), it is submitted that to achieve this by excluding the category of disputes with officers from arbitration was undesirable and that both situations could have been provided for.

The Prescribed Parties in Their Capacities as Such

This is not a requirement laid down by the Acts, nor one prescribed by the Rules. It has nevertheless been annexed judicially to the provisions of the section. The problem arises in situations such as that in *Lukenya Ranching & Farming Co-operative Society Limited v. Kavoloto (1970) E.A. 414:* an employee of a society, who is also a member, is dismissed wrongfully and sues the society for wages and damages for wrongful dismissal. Can the society resist the court's jurisdiction on the ground that this is a dispute between a society and a member (which are prescribed parties) and therefore should be referred to the Registrar? What has happened is that the requirements of the section have been met literally: there is a dispute, it concerns the business of the society, and it is between the prescribed parties. But the courts have not considered this sufficient compliance and have posed the question thus: "Therefore the question is whether or not, although the dispute literally falls within the actual words of the section, it is within the meaning of it."[12] An early case established the distinction in this fashion:

On consideration we are of opinion that, if any other rule be established than this, that matters in difference between the society and its members, in the character of members, can alone be referred to arbitration; if we go one step beyond that, then extraneous matters of any kind, which happen to be in dispute between the society and any of its members, ought to be the subject of a reference. It appears to us, therefore, that the words "matters in dispute" must be read "matters in dispute between the society and its members as members", and not in any other capacity.[13]

This was also the view taken in the *Lukenya Ranching* case. The High Court rejected the society's arguments for arbitration by holding that "The Plaintiff is suing the defendant society not as a member but as an ex-employee, his status of member, *qua* the suit, being in my opinion merely coincidental".[14] The Court of Appeal for East Africa upheld this, saying,

Admittedly the respondent was a member of the society but the present dispute is between the respondent as an employee of the society and the society. The dispute has nothing to do with his membership and his membership is not relevant to this dispute, which is only in relation to his position as employee, that is, as manager of the farm ((1970) E.A. at 419).

The judicial accretion then is this: it is not enough that the section is literally satisfied; for the dispute to fall within its scope, the parties thereto must acquire that status in their character of prescribed parties. In other words, "The grounds of the Plaintiff's action must be that he is injured by the acts in question in his capacity as a member of the society."[15] This, say the courts, is "the true meaning of the rule", this is "the meaning" of the section. Therefore disputes between, for example, member and society in their capacities respectively of landlord and tenant, mortgagor and mortgagee, victim and tortfeasor or seller and buyer of produce not dealt with by the society would not be disputes covered by the section and would not be referred to the Registrar for arbitration, notwithstanding that they apparently fall within the section's provisions. Employer and employee disputes would likewise be excluded, save in Uganda.

"Shall Be Referred to the Commissioner or Registrar"

The basic principle is that recourse to the courts for the settlement of disputes or the determination of rights is so fundamental a safeguard that the presumption of its continued availability is never easily displaced. Therefore it has been a general rule of long standing that "the jurisdiction of superior courts is not taken away, except by express words or necessary implication".[16] Additionally, such words are strictly construed and any ambiguity in their meaning is resolved in favour of the courts retaining jurisdiction.

But it is now well established that, where a statute has provided for the determination of certain disputes by arbitration, the jurisdiction of the courts is ousted.[17] The provisions of the Co-operative Societies Acts that we have examined constitute an ouster of the courts' jurisdiction by necessary implication. These provisions constitute such an ouster and do not merely provide an alternative mode of dispute settlement. Nor do they constitute a delay of the right of action until the specified machinery has been exhausted or been prevented from operating. The words "shall be referred" are mandatory,[18] the courts may not adjudicate on the dispute and other modes of settlement are barred without the consent of all parties. But it must be noted that the exclusion of the courts can only be effected by or with the authority of an Act of Parliament itself. Subordinate legislation, such as the Co-operative Societies Rules, may not effect such exclusion in the absence of express authorization in the principal Act. Such authorization exists in the Tanzanian Act, where the exclusion has in fact been prescribed by the Rules. Such exclusion would therefore be even more inoperative, if it were to be derived solely from the by-laws of a society. It is usual for by-laws to contain such provisions for the settlement of disputes, but one must be clear that they constitute at best a reminder of the provisions of the Act of Parliament and do not of themselves exclude the courts. And this is so notwithstanding that the Rules permit them to provide for the settlement of disputes.

The Prescribed Modes of Settlement of Disputes

Once a dispute under the provisions of the Acts has come into being and has been referred to the Commissioner or Registrar, the Acts prescribe the modes that are to be employed in its settlement. In Tanzania, the Registrar may either decide the dispute himself or he may refer it to arbitration under the Arbitration Ordinance, Cap. 15. In Kenya, the Commissioner has no power to determine the dispute himself but must refer it to an arbitrator appointed by him. But "where any of the parties insist upon being represented by an advocate", the Commissioner may refuse to act under the Co-operative Societies Act, in which case the dispute shall be determined by a single arbitrator under the Arbitration Act, Cap. 49. In Uganda, the Registrar may either decide the dispute himself or refer it for disposal to arbitrators. If a point of law arises in a dispute he has decided to settle himself, he may refer it to the High Court for its decision, which shall form part of the award of the Registrar. An arbitrator may likewise refer any point of law to the High Court for its decision. In Kenya and Uganda, the Rules prescribe the manner in which the reference to the Registrar may be made and it is well to remember that, if the reference to the arbitrator does not comply with those rules, his appointment may be held to be a nullity (see *Masaka District Growers Co-operative Union v. Mumpiwakoma Co-operative Society Limited* (1968) E.A. 630).

Other Modes of Dispute Settlement

Surcharge. The Acts have also provided means other than arbitration for the settlement of disputes. In particular, disputes arising from claims by the society against officers or managers for financial loss have now been better provided for by the inclusion in the Acts of a power vested in the Registrar to surcharge parties connected with the running of a society. It must appear that such loss has been occasioned to the society and there must be an inquiry into the offending conduct. Thereafter, where appropriate, the Registrar may order the party concerned to repay or restore the money or property concerned to the society, together with interest and, it is submitted, the costs of such inquiry and order. The obvious advantage of the surcharge machinery is that the Registrar's order is enforceable summarily by civil process and applies notwithstanding that the action complained of may also constitute a criminal offence. This in practice means that the recovery process by the society in a civil court need not await either police investigation or the determination of a criminal prosecution, contrary to the usual rule of law.[19] No procedure has been prescribed for the Registrar's inquiry and it is submitted that any informal procedure would suffice in assisting the Registrar in arriving at his decision, provided that it complies with the principles of natural justice, for example, both parties to the dispute must be heard and adequate opportunity must be given to each to reply to the case of the other.[20] The surcharge sections, though from the society's viewpoint potentially the ideal provisions to utilize, have not, for several reasons, been invoked as often as they could be and they await a more useful future.

Criminal prosecutions. Criminal prosecutions, too, constitute the determination of certain types of disputes in co-operative societies, in addition to their more usual penal function. Prosecutions may arise out of the offences prescribed by the general criminal law or may arise out of the specific offences created by the Co-operative Societies Acts. The function of a criminal prosecution is also envisaged as assisting in the *prevention* of disputes, as contrasted with their settlement. Convictions are seen to be deterrents to other officers or committees from not complying with the provisions of the law in the discharge of their duties. This may be gathered, for example, from the action of Tanzania in specifying stealing by a servant from a co-operative society as a scheduled offence under its Minimum Sentences Act, 1963, thereby prescribing a heavier minimum penalty.

Inquiries and investigations. Inquiries and investigations initiated by the Registrar under the powers given to him under the Acts have also been utilised in the settlement of disputes in societies, and in particular, unions. The inquiries and investigations do not of themselves decide matters but enable the Registrar to apply his other powers to regularize the state of affairs that has given rise to the conflict and the inquiry. These powers have often been used where the dispute provisions are manifestly inadequate or where political considerations have required inquiry by third parties.

The Policy of the Law

We have seen that specified methods of settling disputes in co-operative societies have been provided. What then is the purpose of Parliament in excluding the courts of law and imposing arbitration and other methods? The intention of the legislation has been held to "save persons concerned from protracted expensive and ruinous litigation in civil courts"[21] and to protect the funds of poor contributors. It is obvious that parties of limited means who band together in co-operative enterprises for the promotion of their economic interests are ill-equipped to embark on long and expensive litigation. It is equally desirable that other and swifter compulsory means should be provided. The courts have remarked that, were every member entitled to sue every committee member or trustee, no person would fill any of the latter gratuitous offices in a society. That is the justification in law. But the exclusion of the courts is also implied by the human investment that co-operation demands. As was said in *Kamta Prasad v. Registrar of Co-operative Societies M.P.* A.I.R. (1967) Madh. Pra. 211, "the co-operative movement is a great moral one" and it is necessary that disputes therein be determined in a manner that does not permanently damage relationships between parties who are to remain members of the same society after the dispute.

That this is the intent of the legislature is borne out by the categories of prescribed parties. Disputes between the participants in the co-operative movement are the only protected disputes. Disputes between co-operators and outsiders are determined by the normal modes, including access to the courts. In furtherance of this is the judicial interpretation of the word "member" in such sections discussed above. Courts have long elaborated that it is not enough to satisfy the excluding provisions that the parties are in fact members or prescribed parties. For the provisions to operate, the dispute must relate to their capacity as such. The benefit of the prescribed machinery is to be enjoyed by co-operators only, and that only when the dispute relates to their status as such. If such interpretation were not given to the provisions, the right to recourse to the courts would be avoided by unscrupulous parties, who would find the price of one share in a society a cheap shield against the rigours of the courts of law.

The background of our legislation[22] has therefore, until recently, taken it for granted that it is desirable and good co-operative law to exclude the courts. We turn below to an examination of the question whether this is a wholly desirable state of affairs.

Is Ouster of the Courts Desirable?

We have seen in the above consideration of why the courts have been excluded that it is felt that there are very real disadvantages in allowing co-operators to have recourse to the courts. It is, however, submitted here that, despite these, there is a strong case for offering the courts as a forum for the settlement of disputes.

The arbitration machinery provided in the Acts does not in practice manifest the benefits of the arbitration process—speed, minimization of costs, and privacy. This is due to two factors. First, the lack of manpower in the co-operative departments and other government agencies; second, the provision, as in Kenya, of alternative modes where parties are represented or where, as in Uganda, though legal representation is forbidden before the Registrar and the arbitrator, recourse may be had to the courts to decide points of law.

Basically, the departments simply do not have enough qualified officers to implement their programme and powers. Still less can they spare them to be diverted into time-consuming tasks which are not creative. Liquidation duties are such an exercise. Settlement of disputes is another. Such a shortage of personnel and ordering of priorities inevitably create a backlog in dealing with disputes. This is further compounded by the frequency of disputes arising from bad management by co-operators and insufficient supervision by government officers. Complaints and disputes go unattended. The result is that disputes are seldom dealt with quickly, and one of the principal benefits of arbitration, namely, speed, is lost. In fact, in *Republic v. The Commission for Co-operative Development ex parte Kabuthi* (1969) E.A. 168, three co-operators applied to the High Court for an order of mandamus to compel the Commissioner to appoint an arbitrator or refuse to act. They had referred a dispute to him in August 1967. No step was taken for a year, until finally, in July 1968, the applicants brought the matter to court. The Commissioner was successful in opposing the issue of the order asked for, but he did not go wholly unscathed. The court remarked on the delay:

> But that the Commissioner allowed the matter to drag on for months is, to my mind, indefensible. He thought he had a duty to perform and it is for comment that, instead of doing what he thought the law required him to do, he felt it necessary to oppose this application instead.

The court then proceeded to deprive him of his costs in these words:

> Each party will bear its own costs. The applicants sent their reference to a public officer, who, they were entitled to assume, knew his duty. He, apart from the great and unwarranted delay, led them to believe they had taken the right course. They then took what appeared to be the only procedure open to them, after which

the Commissioner, for the first time, took the point that there was no dispute under the Act.

Secondly, the fact that parties may opt for representation removes the other advantage of arbitration—the minimization of costs. Arbitration will not cost very much less if both parties are being represented by counsel. Additionally, the other supposed disadvantage of the courts, delay, also manifests itself here. Where the parties are represented, the Commissioner seeks a legally qualified person to be the arbitrator, usually state counsel from the Attorney-General's chambers. Once again, it is not easy to spare counsel for such tasks as frequently as such disputes arise. Again, there is a delay and its attendant backlog.

It must further be kept in mind that, if the act of the parties in having representation results in the adjudication of the dispute by a legally qualified person, then that is not very different from it being adjudicated upon in the courts. It cannot be seriously questioned that the courts are better equipped to sit in judgement on disputed claims than even legally qualified persons who do not have more than a haphazard experience of judicial decision-making. For, as was said, "The proper tribunals for the determination of legal disputes in this country are the courts, and they are the only tribunals which, by training and experience, and assisted by properly qualified advocates, are fitted for the task."[23] Thus, it may be seen that in practice the arbitration machinery provided has not been as advantageous as it might have been expected to be. On the other hand, it is submitted, permitting access to the courts may have certain more positive advantages.

Firstly, open recourse to the courts may mitigate against the excesses of the sort of situation Göran Hyden has expressed fears of. He writes:[24]

> Almost everywhere in Kenya, co-operative leaders are drawn from the economically stronger members of local communities. Ordinary peasants are under the domination of more successful villagers, some of whom are deeply involved in non-agricultural activities. Besides individuals with large holdings, teachers and traders frequently perform leadership roles in rural co-operatives. Indeed, the tendency for co-operatives to serve as stepping-stones for more

ambitious persons rather than as vehicles of progress for the rural "proletariat" is not confined to Kenya. For instance, two Tanzanian studies[25] also indicate that local notables very often assume leadership positions in co-operatives. And such individuals frequently tend to use their position to further personal ambitions and interests. ... co-operatives will continue to come under the influence of those individuals who occupy key economic positions in local communities. Thus, co-operatives will increasingly serve the private interests of powerful local notables rather than the collective welfare of their larger membership. Where conflicts arise between co-operatives and such individuals, we should not expect them to be resolved in favour of the former. Because of the dominance of kinship ties over perceived economic interests, and because of the relative weakness and vulnerability of co-operatives in many areas, we should not expect them to battle effectively with local notables.

If the Department and the Commissioner are helpless to prevent the continued exploitation of the ordinary member by a committee composed of leading persons in the neighbourhood, it is unlikely, in the event of a dispute arising between them, that the Department will be significantly more effective by being the party called upon to determine the dispute. And this despite the drastically enhanced powers given to the Commissioner under the 1966 Act.

Secondly, with the enhanced powers mentioned above laid down by the law, it is questionable whether arbitration by an appointee of the Commissioner can be seen to be a fair and impartial remedy by the ordinary member. For the Commissioner is empowered to appoint as a sole arbitrator an officer of the Department and this is often done. To an aggrieved member complaining about the committee, this is, in effect, an appeal to the very party he is complaining of. For the dispute has arisen despite the wide supervisory powers vested in the co-operative officer and possibly because of the lack of exercise of those very powers or because of their inefficient application. If the determination of the dispute in favour of the member involves making an unfavourable finding in respect of any of the Department's officers, this would be a factor adverse to a satisfactory conclusion being arrived at. In such a situation, the already heavily-weighing political considerations mentioned above, of which the Department complains, would compound an already delicate situation. "Local notables" inevitably happen to be "political notables" and the Department would be hesitant to take upon itself again the role of seeming to oppose the political thinking in that area. Again, because many politicians do see the Department in this role. Would it not be better that a more independent alternative were available? Separate from the Department and more certainly seen to be beyond the reach of the more obvious political pressure?

Thirdly, access to the courts will assist in taking some of the load off a badly overburdened Department. This would free it to concentrate its energies and limited manpower on more productive work. The Department would also be glad to be released from involvement in local politics. The unwelcome attentions mentioned above are generally attracted in disputes which are satisfied in any event by calling in some third party to hold an inquiry or investigation which provides either an independent or a convenient recommendation. While access to the courts is not yet available, it may be more profitable for the Department to free its officers from such work, by relying for available arbitrators on a panel of advocates compiled in consultation with the Law Society. This would not break any new ground, for the Departments have used advocates before and have long relied upon a panel of private accountants and utilized them when the government audit machinery could not cope. It may also be mentioned here that the task of sorting out claims and achieving some degree of finality in the disputed affairs of a society would be made easier if a limitation period were enacted barring claims submitted after the prescribed period. At present claims relating to events which happened five years, and more, ago are often submitted, making a thorough decision an almost impossible task.

Fourthly, permitting access to the courts will move the co-operative movement a little away from its too-close involvement with the Government. As long as the Government remains the arbiter of all disputes in the co-operative movement, so long will the movement continue to be dependent on the Government. Both in the day-to-day administration and in the financial management and requirements, the apron strings are much too tight. Both sides lament this. The movement resents the controls but is resigned to them. The Government protests that such measures are only a temporary educational phase. Despite these latter protestations, it would be optimistic to think in terms of a deadline after which the Government will give up all its controlling powers. As Helm has put it:[26]

> Experience has shown, especially in developing countries, that the civil service is often reluctant to give up an established position. This reluctance is manifested in stereotyped assertions to the effect that the co-operative organisation cannot yet manage on its own. Without pressure from the movement itself, the situation tends to be perpetuated.

What can be done to accelerate that slow process, and certainly lessen the moral dependence of the co-operators on the state, is the removal of the settlement of disputes from the control of the Department. For as long as two parties need a third to determine their differences, so long will the third party wield influence over them. If the Government is sincere in its desire to see a healthy movement, independent of itself, then it must encourage the utilization, if not of other means alone, certainly of alternative means. The courts of law provide such an alternative.

There is also another alternative, and one which would exert the kind of pressure Helm mentions. Ideally, what the co-operative movement needs for the settlement of disputes is a forum within itself. Such a forum would not have the shortcomings of the legal process and would also be free from government attachment. Such body or tribunal could comprise non-officials drawn from the co-operative movement, assisted possibly by a legally qualified person. It could have either original jurisdiction or be an appellate body sitting to consider the arbitrator's decision.

The establishment of such a domestic tribunal would also militate against the harmful effects of the current legislation and its predecessors. For when such wide-ranging controlling powers are contained in the Acts, it is not surprising that the result is a deterioration in co-operative effort and, particularly, management. This is a situation created by the Acts themselves and is clearly noticeable in the matter of disputes. When such supervisory and managerial powers are vested in the Government, it would be unusual, when things began to go wrong, if the member did not think that it was the Government's responsibility, and not his, to straighten things out. He is so used to seeing the Government doing everything for the co-operative anyway. A tribunal of this sort would force upon the societies more active involvement in an area affecting their rights and finances.

Such a tribunal would also bring about a re-assessment by the movement and the Departments of the purpose of co-operative law. Because the current leadership of both the co-operative movement and the Government departments was nurtured in the 1945–6 Ordinances and their thoughts are determined by reference to it, it is specially necessary to break the 1945 mould and to begin anew consideration of the requirements of co-operative legislation. It is necessary to reconsider the effects on co-operators and on the movement not just of such laws but of the attitudes implicit therein. The Ordinances have perpetuated a belief that the remedy for the ills of the movement is another dose of Gvernment interference—only increased. A tribunal of the above sort would correct the emphasis and confirm that the true remedy is increasing involvement by members in the running of their society and by the leaders in the direction of the movement. They would have an opportunity to shape that course through such a tribunal.

However, in the absence of such a body, official or even voluntary, it is submitted that permitting access to the courts will lessen the present dependence of the movement on the Government.

Though delay is an almost inevitable concomitant of court litigation, it is a fault more noticeable in the urban areas and in the higher courts. The lowest subordinate courts, which cover the country better and to which co-operators are nearer, would almost certainly dispose of a case faster than the Department. In any event, it must be remembered that the award of an arbitrator is only enforceable through a court of competent jurisdiction. All the above considerations would, it is submitted, constitute good grounds for permitting access to the courts. The early general wiews regarding exclusion of these disputes from the courts no longer hold. Ugandan legislation, for instance, now provides that, in addition to references by the Registrar and the arbitrator on points of law, any debt arising out of financial loss shall not be the subject of settlement by the Registrar but shall be referred by him to a competent court for settlement (Section 73 (13), Act 30 of 1970).

Conclusions

In this paper the following proposals have been argued:

(*a*) That access to the courts of law should be permitted in the settlement of disputes;

(*b*) That, alternatively or additionally, a co-operative tribunal comprising non-government members should be established to settle disputes;

(*c*) That a panel of advocates available and willing to act as arbitrators should be drawn up in conjunction with the local Law Society and utilized for arbitrations, thus freeing co-operative officers for more creative tasks; and

(*d*) That a period of limitation should be imposed upon the time within which a dispute may be referred to the Registrar under the Acts.

Shem E. Migot-Adholla

The Politics of Mechanization in Sukumaland

The term co-operative has been so widely and differently used that to-day it can be made to apply to a wide range of organizations. It is generally agreed, however, that co-operatives are social movements as well as economic enterprises (often in this order) and that each of these factors is an important ingredient of co-operative organizations. Yet it would appear that the discussion of co-operative efficiency has often tended to emphasize the economic at the expense of the social factors.[1] If, on the whole, in the study of co-operatives in eastern Africa, perhaps undue emphasis has been placed on the economic efficiency of these institutions, this needs to be understood in terms of their historical and philosophic origins in the colonial context. The historical antecedents of agricultural co-operatives in East Africa suggest that co-operation is a creature of social control rather than economic competition. For, in the colonial context, the primary concern of the people who formulated co-operative laws was not with vague notions of economic democracy but rather with law and order, with revenue collection and with the promotion of some selected export crops, for which proper grading and quality control was important—usually necessitating a single-channel market structure.

It is hardly necessary to point out that, on the whole, these notions have not been completely changed. Much of the legislation on co-operatives to-day is largely a carry-over from the colonial laws, with minor amendments, generally of an

---

Shem E. Migot-Adholla is a graduate of the University of Dares-Salaam and is currently writing his Ph.D. thesis at the Department of Agricultural Economics at Michigan State University.

administrative nature. Despite the widely publicized proclamation over much of Africa about the new reliance on co-operatives as an instrument of social and economic reform in the rural areas, it would appear that there has been a reluctance in actual practice to move from mere rhetoric to concrete policy, with the provision of the necessary institutional changes that would enable the co-operatives to perform their proclaimed role. While this remains the general case, certain exceptions can readily be seen in a number of countries. Thus, even within the limited confines of East Africa, co-operatives are no longer identical organizations from one country to another.

The discussion of efficiency in co-operatives must obviously take into consideration the effectiveness of their goal achievement within the community in which they are located. Yet these are very complex and elusive notions. Should the co-operative be judged to be efficient when it helps the peasant to increase his profit margin or when it maintains his loyalty and makes him a "better" member of the corporate community? Since the perception of goals often changes, as co-operatives develop from the spontaneous *mass movements* which characterized their beginnings to the relatively more "rationalistic" *economic organizations* (which they are expected to be today), the measure of efficiency or effectiveness must also change. Yet the perception of goals by the members (insiders) may not always coincide with that of non-members (outsiders). Further more, since the day-to-day operation of the co-operatives is partly a function of governmental control, the performance of those government officers directly concerned with co-operatives must also be evaluated, with a view to determining their efficiency in assisting the co-operatives to realize their goals. Obviously these are problems with much wider implications and cannot be summarily dealt with in a short seminar paper. I shall be concerned here with the divergences between the goals perceived by members of the co-operative and by members of the general public and the goals contained in government policy, as represented in official documents and in the laws and regulations enumerating the functions of co-operatives and providing the procedures for their operations.

But, first, a word about the study of organizational goals. One major criticism of studies which use the realization of goals as the measure of efficiency is that they are often stereotyped. That is, they make their findings dependent on some ideal typical assumptions. Consequently, many such studies find that the organizations are inefficient, since they do not often realize their proclaimed goals. It is worth noting, however, that the same organizations may have some undeclared goals, which should also be taken into consideration in determining their efficiency. In any case, the determination of organizational goals can become a very treacherous exercise, especially where the "insiders" in the organization have goals which may be different from those of the "outsiders". For instance, farmers in a co-operative organization may perceive the goal of such an organization as assisting them to realize the maximum profits from their produce. The management of the same organization may see their goal as being the maximization of the operational margins for the "business", possibly enabling further investment. The government officials, on the other hand, may expect co-operatives to facilitate the proper collection, grading and marketing of crucial export crops. Obviously, these goals are all interdependent. Yet the emphasis on one goal to the exclusion of others can make a lot of difference in assessing efficiency or inefficiency.

The present paper is concerned with the realization of goals in a very mundane and practical way, namely, the operational efficiency of the tractor enterprise organized by the Victoria Federation of Co-operative Unions (VFCU; Nyanza Co-operative Union (NCU) after November 1967).[2] Specifically, I shall concentrate on the effects of the institutional structure of the co-operative organization, as well as the dynamics of local social and political relations (including governmental relations), on both the efficiency and the effectiveness of the project. It may be useful to state this concern in the form of some generalized questions:

1. Was the institutional organization of the VFCU conducive to the utilization of tractors, so that their use could be profitable?

2. Was the use of tractors beneficial to a significant proportion of the peasant members of the co-operative organization?

3. Was the tractor operation satisfactory in the eyes of the government and the general population?

4. Which social groups actually determined the way the tractor enterprise was operated and how did they do this?

These are some of the more important questions that are investigated in this paper. No pretence is made of providing answers to all of them, nor is a full answer given to any specific question. The overriding purpose of this paper is to illustrate how difficult it is for a co-operative organization to set goals for itself and to realize them in an environment which includes other powerful groups with different, if not antagonistic interests. In attempting to deal with the broad questions stated above, no effort is made to handle each question in isolation. Thus, the answers to the questions evolve in the course of the analysis. No suggestions are made as to how to re-organize the co-operatives in order to achieve maximum efficiency or effectiveness. These will be found in the reports of the various study groups which deliberated during the course of the seminar.

The Organization of the Tractor Enterprise

In 1964 the Government of Tanzania launched an extensive mechanization experiment, in which some co-operative unions were provided with tractors under loan arrangements. It was not clear at the time whether the experiment had been motivated by a desire to promote mechanized cultivation as such or to increase the agricultural output by extending the acreage cultivated. The tractors were deployed without prior consideration of their utility in different areas. For example, there were tractors in such areas as Bukoba, where the high slopes and the hilly terrain and indeed the rich growth of weeds, such as couch grass, made cultivation by hand almost imperative. There cannot be any doubt now that the tractor project had not been properly conceived. Yet it is sad to note that, when the project was finally terminated, it was the co-operatives (and ultimately the peasants) who were made to bear all the costs, while some of the "planistrators"[3] who may have initiated it in the first place had perhaps been rewarded by higher promotions. But such is the irony of bureaucratic immunity in a situation in which the peasants and their ignorance provide a convenient scapegoat. I shall return to this subject later in the paper.

Under this tractor project, the VFCU received nearly 300 tractors equipped with disc ploughs. These tractors were then distributed to the 20 unions scattered over Sukumaland and other neighbouring districts. This brief account is concerned with the tractors managed by the Kilagabageni Union (now the Sola Zone). When the co-operative organization acquired its first fleet of tractors, there appears to have been very little prior examination of how the existing organizational structure could be adapted for their efficient operation. Nor was the ultimate responsibility for such efficiency clearly determined. Initially, the tractors were considered the sole responsibility of the VFCU, and a new Tractor Department was created at the head office in Mwanza. Tractor units were also established at the unions under the direction of a supervisor, responsible (in theory) to the manager at the head office. The unit supervisor was responsible for the general administration and maintenance of the fleet of tractors, the maintenance of accounts and other records in respect of the tractor operations, and the supervision of the drivers and the unit mechanic in his charge.

However, at the union, the supervisor's responsibilities were usurped, for the union manager remained supreme. As the most senior officer at that level, the union manager exercised overall control over all union employees—which the supervisor, the mechanic and the drivers all were. The union itself was nearly a semi-autonomous entity, under the overall direction of an elected executive committee, which had powers to hire and fire any of the employees—with the exception, perhaps, of the manager. It is clear enough that the weak integration of the new Tractor Department as a parallel line of command to the existing structure of the co-operative organiza-

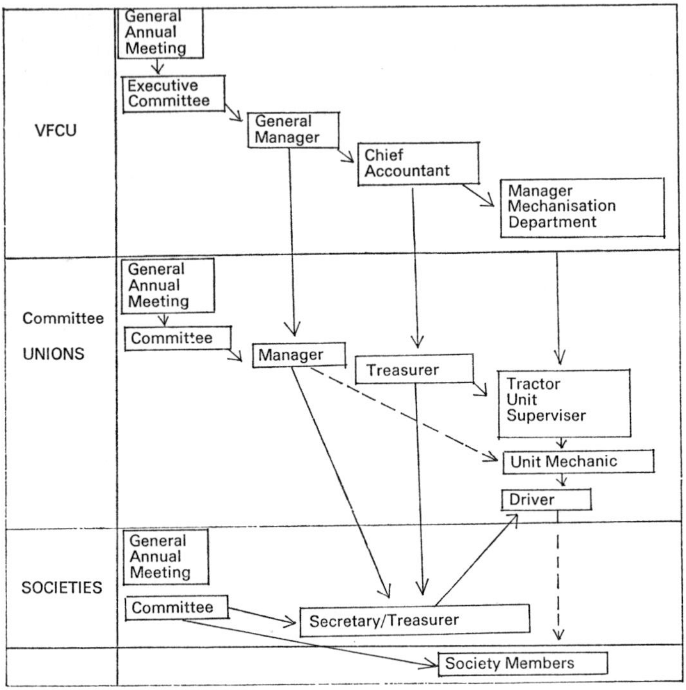

Fig. 1. *Structural diagram showing the chain of authority in the tractor enterprise of the Victoria Federation of Co-operative Unions* (the direction of the arrows shows the direction of authority in the hierarchy).

tion introduced a number of ambiguities, particularly at the union level. Although the supervisor was accountable for the operation of the tractors, he lacked real power by which to carry out the duties assigned to him. The drivers could only be hired and fired by the committee of locally elected notables, who, because they were elected, were often motivated by considerations of political expediency rather than day-to-day operational efficiency. Fig. 1 shows the hierarchy of authority within the co-operative organization and how the Mechanization Department was grafted on to the existing structure.

When the tractor project was started, the Kilagabageni Union received seven Fordson Major tractors. Eight Massey-Ferguson tractors were added early in 1966. All the tractors were equipped with disc ploughs, but the first lot had also been accompanied by five-ton trailers. The provision of only seven trailers became a potential source of driver discontent and administrative wrangling, for it meant that only seven drivers would be working during the season when no ploughing was done. Since each of the drivers was assigned a specific tractor, this implied that driver assignment to a Fordson Major became an extra privilege, the management of which was contested between the manager of the Union, the unit supervisor and even members of the executive committee. It has not been possible to obtain data for determining the relative efficiency of tractors in ploughing and haulage work. Records of ploughing, haulage or fuel consumption were hardly kept. Although each driver had been provided with a record book for the purpose, it would appear that the literacy requirement for all the drivers was not properly fulfilled at Kilagabageni, for the drivers were unable to keep any usable records. However, the lack of records was ultimately the result of defective supervision—at all levels of the operation, in both the co-operative organization and the relevant government agency.[4]

Let us briefly examine some of the personnel at Kilagabageni who were directly involved in the tractor project. The unit supervisor, although lacking even the barest knowledge of motor mechanics, had a fairly ample experience of co-operative management. Before assuming his current position, he had been employed by the Union as Co-operative Education Officer. He had also previously worked in various capacities in primary societies, one of these being secretary/treasurer. His job experience also included working as a tax clerk for the Maswa District Council, a post he left after allegations of embezzlement brought against him ended in an unsuccessful court action. The unit supervisor had had a formal education of eight years and a number of short courses in co-operative management at the Co-operative College in Moshi.

The personal relationship between the supervisor and his closest work-mate, the unit mechanic, was not particularly friendly. At the time of our investigation, the supervisor was writing applications for jobs in clerical positions at the co-operative headquarters in Mwanza and in the local government offices. He considered the wages at Kilagabageni too low for his level of education, especially when they were compared with the money the mechanic was making in his "moonlight" repair work on privately owned tractors in the area. The mechanic at Kilagabageni had gained considerable experience, as he had worked for three years in a workshop at Mwanza where Massey-Ferguson tractors were being assembled. Although he had had only six years of formal education, his knowledge of tractor mechanics was admirable. He knew the tractor parts at sight but could hardly recognize their technical names in English. Thus, between the supervisor and the mechanic the proper control of spare parts was largely a matter of informed guesswork.

Given the general ignorance of machinery among rural people in eastern Africa and especially the lack of experience with tractors in Sukumaland, it can be seen how minor repair work on the privately owned machines became a very lucrative enterprise. At the time of this study, there were more than 240 privately owned tractors in Maswa District alone. Yet the nearest servicing and repair service provided by the commercial dealers was in Mwanza, about 100 miles away. Most mechanics in the area thus had a ready source of extra income. The unit mechanic at Kilagabageni was well respected for his proficiency, especially by some members of the executive committee, who also operated their own commercial tractor-hire service. Often he repaired such tractors on the co-operative premises—using the facilities and tools in the Union workshop. There is no proof that co-operatively owned spare parts were used on such jobs, but the possibility is not remote.

Kilagabageni was especially fortunate to have, within immediate call, the services of the Field Mechanization Officer from the Ministry of Agriculture. The Mechanization Officer at the time of the survey had received a fairly adequate training for his work. Having completed eight years of formal primary education and one year of secondary school, he was trained in general mechanics at the Moshi Trade School for two years. Following this, he spent another two years at the Dar-es-Salaam Technical College, where he learned agricultural mechanics. Upon completion of the course, he was assigned to the Ministry of Agriculture and sent to the Ukiriguru Agricultural Research Station for a three-month course on the economics of farm mechanization. He was then seconded for a month respectively to the Prdoch and Motor Mart workshops in Mwanza to familiarize himself with the repair and maintenance procedures for Fordson and Massey-Ferguson tractors, the two models largely operating in Sukumaland. When the Field Mechanization Officer was finally posted to Mwanza, it is clear that he had been very well prepared—technically.

Once in the field, the elaborate technical training and experience of the Mechanization Officer was very little utilized. Yet this cannot be said to be an isolated case. It is a patent fact that most professional field officers spend much of their time in government offices rather than in the field. Indeed, the provison of transport facilities and the requirements for the fulfilment of certain routine (bureaucratic) duties make this imperative. Furthermore, so much concern with the promotion of technical innovations rather than with the "education" of the farmers (i.e. concentration on the "clients") causes the extension officers to concentrate their attention on the innovative clients, thus neglecting the majority of their potential clients. A combination of many of these factors helped to bring about a closer working relationship between the Field Mechanization Officer assigned to Maswa District and the tractor operation at Kilagabageni. The Union premises were only two miles from the District Agricultural Office, and the tractors were normally kept at the Union, except during cultivation periods. In addition, it was fairly easy to make the tractor drivers employed by the Co-operative Union attend the short courses organized by the Mechanization Officer as a condition of their employment. Because of the wide dispersal of privately owned machines, the drivers hardly ever attended these courses, nor were they reached in the field by the Mechanization Officers.

During the survey period, it appeared that the Mechanization Officer had almost no work to do. The department's funds for transportation had run out, so that he could not even visit the other VFCU tractor units, the nearest of which was only 12 miles away. To my knowledge, no courses for drivers were organized that year, despite the overall increase of the number of tractors in the district. But although the pace of work was exceedingly relaxed, not all the officers spent their time idly. Some of the more enterprising engaged in repairing privately owned tractors—for cash payment, sometimes during the normal office hours. One of the ablest Field (Mechanization) Officers in the district established a commercial venture, operating a little retail shop near the Co-operative Union premises, at the same time as he was putting up a more prestigious building for the same operation—no doubt encouraged by his "moonlight" prospects.

But the commercial operations of this government-employed Field Mechanization Officer are not an isolated case. It appeared to be the practice that other government extension officers usually visited the relatively well-off farmers. On the face of it, this would seem to be a case of the concentration of extension effort where there was, at least, some likelihood of a favourable response. This appears to be the idea behind the "better-farmer" or improvement approach to agricultural development. But there are also indications that extension officers paid particular attention to certain individuals who provided lavish meals, drinks and other entertainment. Some such farmers even offered the government officers accommodation while on extended field trips. Without knowing whether the farmers offered such "gifts" and services in the expectation of some favour, it would be difficult to characterize such "hospitality" as an example of "corruption". But, of course, one must assume that the extension officers knew what they were not supposed to do, even though the peasants did not.[5]

Co-operative Tractors and Local-level Power Struggle

When the effectiveness of an organization is assessed at a certain specific point in time, the social and non-social environment within which the organization operates must be taken into consideration. Whether the organization has as its goal the production of services for the environment or not, its performance depends in part on the co-operation and goodwill of powerful elements in the environment. Indeed, these forces in the environment often help to make the organization alter its day-to-day operations in some sufficient way, so that it is possible to talk of the organization as having developed some informal or latent goals. In a number of cases, the informal or latent goals may be in sharp contrast to the formal and manifest goals. The way in which the VFCU in general and the tractor project in particular were used to enhance the influence of various persons in the community is such an example.

Obviously the success of the VFCU tractor enterprise depended upon the soundness of the formal procedures intended for its operation. I have already suggested that the newly created Mechanization Department of the VFCU was ill adapted to the existing organization structure. At the actual operational level the tractor project was overloaded with unproductive personnel whose formal roles only helped to generate stress and "institutional suspicion".[6] Informally, though, varying levels of co-operation and collusion were reached by the different actors—for good or for evil.

One role relationship that generated suspicion was that between the tractor driver and the committee-man at the primary society who supervised him daily. The formal procedures were so rigid that they could only be counter-productive. For instance, the driver could not start his daily work until the supervising committee-man had arrived at the society's premises, where, because of insurance regulations, the tractor had to be left overnight. The tractor then travelled "empty" until it reached the field to be cultivated—such fields being always widely scattered. Because they were unionised, the drivers worked a regular eight-hour day, with an hour's break for lunch. But work was defined as driving the tractor, not just ploughing, and the return journey to the society had therefore to be started early, so that the driver was there before the office closed. No minimum ploughing was required and there were no incentives for the proper maintenance of the machines; a bonus of 5 shillings for each acre ploughed above the required 25 acres per month was paid, but no attempt was ever made to assess its aggregate or relative effects, since no records were kept in respect of the costs or productivity of individual tractors or drivers.

Clearly, the drivers did not need to work any more than their "normal" rate, unless they wished to make extra cash by the illegitimate use of the tractors. But, in order to do this, they needed the co-operation of the supervising committee-men. On his part, the committee-man needed the co-operation of the driver, in order to do such favours as offering ploughing services on credit to his neighbouring clientele. After 1965, ploughing on credit was stopped by the VFCU, but in reality the practice continued until the project was discontinued in 1967. There is no doubt that this could only have been possible through some amount of collusion between drivers and the supervising committee-men or total neglect by the committee-men and possibly the secretaries of the primary societies. Indeed, it would appear that nobody really cared much about the economic efficiency of the tractor project—no assessment of marginal returns was ever made throughout the existence of the project by the Mechanization Department of the VFCU, the Co-operative Inspectorate Division or even the Mechanization Division of the Ministry of Agriculture. The statistics collected by all these agencies were often of very little use in economic analysis beyond the making of some very simplistic and impressionistic comparisons.[7]

It is not enough to state that the inefficiencies in the VFCU tractor enterprise were a function of influences in the environment, for that would be to explain away the problem. The project was obviously known to be defective soon after it started, yet nothing was done to correct such deficiencies or to discontinue the project until the end of 1967. Could it have been that it was politically opportune to wait so long? It may not have been known to the manager of the Mechanization Division that the committee-men at the primary society had turned tractor service into an instrument for rewarding political supporters and punishing adversaries, but it certainly was known that the tractors were operating at a loss. Yet even the Union did not act to stop such mismanagement. I suggest that any corrective action on the part of the elected committee-men, both at the Union and the primary society, would not have been in the perceived interests of these same committee-men. I shall illustrate this by one example.

The Kumalija Society, only two miles from the township of Nyalikungu, was considered, at the time of the investigation, to be one of the most successful societies in the whole district. Its committee had remained relatively constant since it was founded in 1958; four members out of the original 10 were still holding their seats in 1968. Except for a lapse of two years, the society had had virtually the same chairman and the founding secretary was also still in office. Starting with a membership of 306 at the time of its registration, the Society had more than tripled in 10 years, having more than 1 035 members. It ranked among the five biggest societies in Maswa District.

When the tractor enterprise was started, an attempt was made at Kumalija to operate on a first-come-first-served basis, but this plan was immediately dropped, as it involved excessive "empty" travelling. An alternative plan was then followed, whereby ploughing was done largely within a single neighbourhood each day. It is not difficult to see that this system was much more favourable to the committee-men, for it meant in effect that they only supervised work in their own neighbourhoods. According to statements made in interviews based on random sample, all the respondents who had used the VFCU tractor services had done so when the tractor was in the charge of a committee-man from their local area. Many of the drivers felt that this practice was exceptionally sound, yet they also conceded that the intimacy between the committee-man and his "clients" presented other problems.

With their close, face-to-face, primary relations, the farmers constitute a well-knit community, in which the exchange of services is little governed by the idea of equality of value. When a person does a good turn to his neighbour, his action is evaluated in terms of social investment. In other words, the person accepting the service also accepts his social "debt" to the giver, although this may not be stated overtly. Obviously, some people are in positions in which they can give more services than they receive in the short run; this gains them social prestige and respect. Now the committee-men of the society found themselves in similar positions—with favours to distribute in the form of tractor services. The way in which they distributed the tractor services could have implications for their tenure of office on the society's committee. It could also have implications for the profitability of the enterprise. A committee-man overseeing tractor cultivation was thus faced with a choice—either to pursue a business-like, formal procedure with his neighbours, as the VFCU regulations demanded, or to maximize their political clientele and brighten their social image within the neighbourhood. Most committee-men decided to follow the latter course.

Earlier, when ploughing on credit was allowed, committee-men would offer these services primarily to their supporters—persons in their immediate neighbourhood. Very often no records of such transactions were kept. According to some government field officers, it would appear that some committee-men treated these "unrecorded" credits as their personal business and pocketed whatever cash they later collected from the "debtors". In some cases, drivers were made to plough gratis for the close friends or relatives of a committee-man. Although promises of payment were often made, the drivers had learned not to take them seriously. Membership of the committee of the primary society was evidently a very lucrative "job", to which many people aspired. Income was raised not only "illegitimately" from the tractors but also from other "legitimate" sources, such as allowances for tractor supervision, duty rounds at the society, and end-of-year bonuses. For almost no productive work at all (except perhaps attendance at several committee meetings and a round of tractor supervision), an ordinary committee-man "officially" drew more than 700 shillings each year.

After the tractor project had been discontinued, one farmer suggested that it was no longer worth while being a committee-man. This emphasizes the "distance" at which the farmers identified themselves with certain operations of the VFCU.

They hardly saw the seamy side of the committee-men's business in terms of injustice, even though they must have known that certain activities were illegal. In circumstances in which a man could secure personal gain by the infringement of some alien regulation, with little chance of detection, the legal technicalities mattered little, especially when the infringement caused no immediate conceivable damage to a member of the relevant community. Although "Victoria", as the Sukumaland co-operative giant was popularly known, was not just an empty idea, it had come to be associated rather vaguely with something that represented a reservoir of benefits, for which many societies and unions were in competition. Such feeling found expression in geographical localism or kinship affiliations. It is conceivable that rather than diminishing the neighbourhood–kinship sectionalism the co-operative organization may have increased it. Thus, it may be argued that class differences within the local neighbourhood–kinship groups played no prominent part in shaping the consciousness of the members of the society. Indeed, some evidence suggest that participation by the peasants in the affairs of their society was very little conditioned by any considerations of socio-economic differences before the Arusha Declaration. But this is not to suggest that the peasants were totally unaware of the differential advantages to individuals or groups of individuals at the society or union level.

In unstructured interviews with members of the Kunalija Society, it was possible to make an assessment of the farmers' perception of the differential influence of certain societies in Kilagabageni Union. A number of farmers had indicated that some societies in the Union were more powerful than others, specifically, they were said to be monopolizing the use of tractors for much longer periods. Asked to name the societies, nearly all the farmers mentioned Ngulinguli, Malita, Masanwa and Isagenghe, in that order. The influence enjoyed by these societies was attributed to the presence of their representatives on the committee of the Union. This interpretation, however, could not be validated by the use of other data, due to the absence of written records. The assertion about the long use of tractors may possibly be maintained only against Ngulinguli (from which the president of the Union came), judging by the remarkably large acreage of tractor cultivation. Or could it have been that the society was just run more efficiently?

Village-level Politics, Party Politics and Government Agencies

One problem posed by the localism of peasants in their attitudes to the co-operative organization is the extent to which such localism impinges on their conscious identification with the wider national society. Another way of stating this problem is to ask about the relationship between the TANU and the co-operative organization, especially as they appear in the perception of the peasants. Naturally, the historical development of the two organizations has quite a lot to do with how they may be perceived today. "If the TANU is truly the farmers' association, as our political leaders say, then why do they allow us to have the co-operative societies?" This rhetorical question explains the feeling of many people at the time that affairs of a political nature (meaning TANU affairs) should not be allowed to interfere with the interests of the co-operatives as the organizations of farmers *qua* farmers. Such a distinction is, however, very difficult to make, especially in view of the extent to which TANU and "Victoria" were interpreted, particularly in their formative years. Perhaps it was not political encroachment, as such, but its perceived disruptive effects that the farmers and their leaders objected to.

It is worth noting that none of the secretaries of the primary societies affiliated to the Kilagabageni Union during 1968 held any official position in the local sub-branches of the TANU. Indeed, it would appear that there was a lack of enthusiasm about party affairs among the general population. Party matters were treated as something alien and separate from the peasants' primary concern with the co-operative. This may have been the result of the peasants' perception of the relative extent to which the two organizations fulfilled their immediate needs. Yet this separation between the political and economic matters is a relatively new phenomenon, for in the formative years of the co-operative organization no such distinction was made.[8] In fact, the people who played a predominant role in mobilizing the membership of the co-operative movement also mobilized for the TANU at the same time.

There is a sense in which the people who provided the link between party and co-operative can also be said to have provided the link between the "traditional" and the "modern" aspects of social and economic life. Most of these people were non-farmers, they were relatively better educated than the rest of the population and all of them had had some experience in an urban job. But they were not so far removed from the rural source as to become alienated. Indeed, it is noteworthy that such men emerged towards the end of the 1960's in leadership positions, both in the party and the co-operative organization. The ambiguous roles of such persons in the party and the co-operatives makes it difficult to assess the parts they played in encouraging (even by benign neglect) the blatant interferences by party and government officials in the tractor enterprise.

I have already referred to practices whereby local co-operative leaders benefitted from the repair and servicing facilities provided by the unit mechanic. Apart from these, certain powerful political and administrative officers benefitted from the tractor services on their own farms. The unit supervisor at Kilagabageni intimated that requests for such "favours" were often very difficult to turn down and that it was sometimes unwise to do so. Thus, although such practices had been severely criticized by the Presidential Commission of 1966, a VFCU tractor had been used to plough some four acres of the private farm of a senior political and administrative officer in Mwanza District.[9]

But more direct and perhaps more damaging to the tractor enterprise was the direct interference in co-operative affairs by political institutions. The co-operative tractors were easily commanded to work on an assortment of projects with dubious economic goals. The extent of the loss to the VFCU tractor project contributed by the various TANU- or TYL-sponsored projects will perhaps never be known. The extent of the loss to the enterprise caused by the Block Farm Experiment has not been accurately established. It was estimated that the Block

Farms owed the VFCU 1.7 million shillings in 1965 alone. The estimate for 1966 is 2 million shillings. These figures include expenses in respect of tractor services, fertilizers, and insecticides, all of which were handled by the Mechanization Department of the VFCU. It is rather ironic to observe that, while the employees in the VFCU associated with the failure of the tractor enterprise were demoted or dismissed in 1967, the government and party officials associated with the Block Farms and their contribution to the ruin of the VFCU may actually have been promoted or rewarded for their enthusiasm!

Conclusion

I have tried in this paper to show how the local-level social and political relationships affect the performance of co-operatives. In this on-going interplay of forces, three factors emerge into prominence: kinship–neighbourhood loyalties, socio-economic differentiation, and political power deriving from bureaucratic appointment. The first two are perhaps the most crucial in the context of peasant politics. These factors influence the participation of peasants and managers alike; they also determine the benefits that each of the categories, either as individuals or as a group, derive from the organization. The fact of differential participation in the co-operative organization obviously raises important questions concerning social accountability or the effectiveness of the organization. However, it does not follow that the ineffectiveness of the co-operative organization automatically results in the economic inefficiency of the organization as a business enterprise. Yet the question of efficiency and social accountability cannot be dismissed lightly. Co-operatives are institutions of vital economic importance; their efficiency therefore becomes a matter of governmental concern. But, if co-operatives are to play a role in rural development, they will also need to be truly democratic. In one sense, democracy implies the ability by the peasants to manage (or mismanage) their own affairs. Obviously, a healthy co-operative policy will have to strike a balance between the two extremes of democracy and efficiency.

It is readily obvious that the discussion of co-operative efficiency in isolation from the total economic and political environment is, at best, futile. I have drawn sufficient examples from the VFCU tractor project to illustrate how the power relationships within the co-operative organization are directly linked with the socio-economic relations in the wider society. Differential participation, manipulation of benefits, etc. are not characteristic only of the co-operative organizations. These are social ills that are often rampant in other segments of society. It would be hypocritical therefore to point to corruption in the co-operatives without showing that it is linked to corruption elsewhere in the society. For if the peasant is to be saved by some sort of socialist ideology, such ideology has to be embraced by the ethnic society.

But a humanistic ideology is not in itself the answer to co-operative inefficiency and ineffectiveness. This should be clear from the long history of co-operative chaos in some of the socialist countries in eastern Europe. It is conceivable that over-zealous implementation and demands for total conformity may stifle local initiative and lead to apathy among the members, causing the co-operative movement to degenerate into a government bureaucracy—cold, distant and indifferent.

Acknowledgements

In preparing this paper, I have tried to leave out much unnecessary "sociologese", in the hope that my thoughts might thereby be made a little clearer. No doubt some of my academic colleagues will find the paper lacking in conceptual and analytical vigour. However, if the practical problems are sufficiently illustrated, we should all be satisfied. The more sociologically inclined reader will find a more engaging version of this study elsewhere.[10]

This paper is based on an earlier, much longer report written in March 1969. The field investigation on which the earlier report was based was carried out in 1968. Further field work was carried out in 1969 after the original paper had been written, and some of the data collected then have been used in the preparation of this paper. The present paper is only presented here for discussion and should not be regarded as final.

I must acknowledge the assistance I received from the Department of Political Science at the University of Dar-es-Salaam, which made possible the preparation of the original paper and subsequent field-work in Sukumaland. I should also like to express my gratitude to Mzee Filipo Ndaki (President) and Mr Idi Mtingwa (General Manager), both of the Nyanza Co-operative Union, all the other persons in the organization and the government officers who, although not mentioned by name, allowed me access to their impressive stores of knowledge of the co-operative movement in Sukumaland, especially in Morena District.

Appendix 1

Table 1. *Tractor Ploughing at Kilagabageni Union for the October 1965 to February 1966 Season.*

	Acreage			Money paid (Shs.)		
Society	Ploughed	Ridged	Harrowed	Cash	Credit	Total
Ngulinguli	252	1	42	11 640	1 005	12 645
Budekwa	147	9	—	7 020	—	7 020
Mahembe	138	—	—	5 400	810	6 210
Walaga	125	11	—	6 120	—	6 120
Kinamweli	103	—	—	4 590	45	4 635
Kumalija	23	60	4	3 855	—	3 855
Lungunano	83	—	2	3 795	—	3 795
Isageng'he	67	15	2	2 490	1 260	3 750
Mwingwa	63	—	—	2 835	—	2 835
Bushitala	62	1	—	2 340	495	2 835
Senani	53	6	—	2 340	315	2 655
Kungusu	43	—	—	1 933	—	1 933
Mgemu	38	5	—	1 933	—	1 933
Kizungu	41	—	—	1 170	675	1 845
Masamwa	20	20	—	1 800	—	1 800
Moalagane	24	15	—	1 260	495	1 755
Kidula	32	—	—	1 440	—	1 440
Kagongolo	21	6	—	1 215	—	1 215
Mwaukoli	20	—	2	960	—	960
Mwanindo	15	4	—	855	—	855
Bulubalo	16	—	—	720	—	720
Mwasange	14	1	—	675	—	675
Sangombe	7	—	—	315	—	315
Ng'wabulaturu	6	—	—	270	—	270
Haloya	2	2	—	180	—	180
Total for Kilagabageni Union	1 415	156	52	67 155	5 100	72 255

Source: *Tractor Report, Kilagabageni*, p. 595.

Table 2. *Tractor Ploughing at Kilagabageni Union for the 1966–67 Season.*

Society	Acreage			All money
	Ploughed	Harrowed	Ridged	paid (Shs.)
Ngulinguli	593	1	—	27 180
Mwingwa	375	—	—	16 875
Malita	343	6	—	15 615
Walaga	284	—	—	12 780
Senani	254	—	—	11 430
Budekwa	240	—	—	10 800
Bulubalo	223	—	—	10 035
Kungusu	196	5	—	9 090
Sengwe	183	—	—	8 235
Sang'ombe	165	—	—	7 425
Masanwa	116	26	—	6 390
Kumalija	140	—	—	6 300
Iyogelo	117	—	—	5 265
Ngwaukoli	107	—	—	4 815
Ngwanyahina	93	—	—	4 185
Ng'wabulaturu	91	—	—	4 095
Isageng'he	78	13	—	4 095
Kizungu	87	—	—	3 915
Busamnda	45	45	—	3 870
Makao	62	—	—	2 790
Semu	48	—	—	2 160
Ngwabusalu	47	—	—	2 115
Lalago	46.5	—	—	2 092.5
Balele	33	13	—	2 070
Ngwaholo	31	—	—	1 395
Iponabolo	16	—	—	720
Bahebe	10	—	—	450
Kilagabageni	1	—	—	45
Total for the Union	4 035.5	99	6	186 232.5

Source: *Tractor Report, Kilagabageni*, pp. 307–308.

Table 3. *Farm Equipment Survey, Maswa District, 14 December 1967.*

Admin. division	Plough	Ox-drawn Ridger	Ox-drawn Cultivator	Ox-drawn Trailer	Plough	Tractor-drawn Ridger	Tractor-drawn Harrower	Tractor-drawn Flour mills	Tractor	Milk separators
Nung'hu	501	1	—	1	9	7	—	—	11	—
Meatu	1 061	—	—	2	31	—	—	11	12	—
Kanadi	257	—	—	—	20	—	—	—	14	2
Itilima	1 869	—	—	5	44	6	—	11	44	—
Ntuzu	1 332	—	2	8	54	—	—	26	54	25
Sengerema	429	—	—	5	44	6	—	13	51	—
Mwagala	3 718	3	5	1	38	—	—	—	14	3
VFCU	—	—	—	16	55	18	2	—	55	—
Total	9 168	3	7	38	295	27	2	61	255	30

Source: District Agricultural Officer,
Maswa, *Mechanization Report*, December 1967.

Table 4. *Privately Owned Tractor Census, Maswa District, 4 January 1968.*

Admin. division	MF	Ford	Fordson S/Major	Ford Major	Nuffield	IH	Ford Extra	FIAT	Total
Nung'hu	9	5	—	—	—	—	—	—	14
Meatu	12	3	—	—	—	—	—	—	15
Kanadi	11	3	—	1	—	—	—	—	15
Itilima	36	4	1	1	—	3	—	1	46
Ntuzu	56	3	2	—	—	—	—	—	61
Sengerema	55	5	8	—	1	—	2	—	71
Mwagala	12	5	1	—	—	—	—	—	17
Total	191	28	12	2	1	3	2	1	239

Source: District Agricultural Officer, Maswa, *Mechanization Report*, December 1967.

Table 5. *Shinyanga Region Co-operative Union's Tractor Ploughing during the 1966–67 Season (in acres).*

Union	Ploughed	Ridged	Harrowed	Total	Tractors	Tractor average
Chenge cha Balimi	2 548	—	—	2 348	16	159·25
Kishampanda	1 239	2	—	1 241	16	77·55
Kilagabageni	4 057·5	99	6	4 172·5	15	277·50
Lukubanija	2 555·5	40	152	2 747·5	15	170.40
Isangijo	1 000	—[a]	—[a]	1 000	14	—[a]
Total	11 400	141	158	11 699	76	154

[a] Report from union incomplete.

Source: *Annual Report (Mechanization)*,
Ministry of Agriculture (Shinyanga), 20 January 1968.

Table 6. *Co-operative Union's Tractor Ploughing, 1965–68, in Shinyanga Region (in acres).*

Union	1965–66	1966–67	1967–68
Chenge cha Balimi	1 959	2 548	855
Kilagabageni	1 623	4 162	2 274
Lukubanija	1 294	2 747	1 222
Isangijo	1 918	1 150[a]	550[a]
Kishampanda	2 334	1 241	448
Total	9 128	11 849	5 350

[a] Estimated acreage.

Source: *Annual Report (Mechanization)*,
Ministry of Agriculture (Shinyanga), 20 January 1968.

Edward Karanja

The Problem of Amalgamating Co-operative Societies—The Case of Northern Tetu

The problems facing the co-operative movement in Kenya are of many kinds and require much understanding and attention in trying to solve them. Many studies so far have dealt with general co-operative-management problems and challenges. However, in the present study I have tried to highlight another important problem, which in past studies has received very little attention. The problem itself is that of trying to amalgamate various existing mono-purpose co-operative societies into viable and larger economic institutions, which is the trend in the country at present. The general belief in such cases is that economic factors must be given priority and that they should determine the shape that such amalgamation should take.

This paper is an attempt to show that there are other non-economic factors which co-operative-society members consider to be just as important as the economic ones in determining the set-up and the amalgamation of their societies. The survey was conducted in November and December 1970, and I am grateful to Dr Ascroft, who advised on the drawing up of the questionnaire, and to Dr Hyden and Dr Chambers, who helped with suggestions, particularly during the analysis of the data.

Edward Karanja, a Research Fellow of the Institute of Development Studies, University of Nairobi, is currently writing his Ph.D. thesis at the Graduate School of Public and International Affairs, University of Pittsburgh.

Organizational Problems

The co-operative movement in Kenya is now 25 years old as an officially recognized movement and has shown tremendous growth since independence. The Kenya Government recognizes the important role that the movement has played in the past and expects it to play a much greater role in the future. This has already been underlined in the country's current Development Plan, which states that "co-operatives have an extremely important role to play, especially in the small-scale farming areas, and the Government intends to intensify its efforts to encourage the healthy development of the co-operative movement".[1] However, the movement has had its share of difficulties, such as poor management, which causes general inefficiency, favouritism towards committee members, misappropriation and misapplication of funds, and lack of business experience on the part of the managing committees.

It was the recognition of these shortcomings in the movement that prompted the Government to enact the Co-operative Societies Act of 1966, with the intention of trying to curb such malpractices. The Government has pledged itself to strengthen and intensify its machinery for guiding, supervising and controlling the movement through the enforcement of this Act. Thus, "the overriding concern of the Government during the next three years is that co-operatives should be disciplined and made to operate more efficiently in accordance with sound business principles".[2]

At the same time, it is important to remember that we cannot discuss the successes and failures of the co-operative societies in a vacuum, without considering their environmental setting and the conditions under which they have to work. Many aspects of the environmental constraints and challenges facing the co-operative movement in East Africa have already been widely discussed in recent works, such as *Co-operatives and Rural Development in East Africa,* edited by C. G. Widstrand, and *African Co-operatives* by Göran Hyden (forthcoming).

However, for the purpose of this study, it is important to highlight the problems which are of specific importance and relevance here. The success or failure of any organization depends for the most part on its ability to utilize its resources in meeting the challenges and constraints presented to it by its environment. This, of course, assumes that, to begin with, such an organization has at the outset spelled out clearly its goals and objectives. If we view the co-operative societies as such, we find that in most cases they lack clear-cut goals and objectives and consequently are unable to manipulate the environment in such a way as to achieve their declared objectives. In such cases, co-operative societies become incapacitated organizations and act like "the blind, groping about in the dark".[3]

Sometimes, where the goals have been well defined, there has been a lack of whole-hearted acceptance of these goals by the members of the co-operative societies. This problem is a critical one, since the end result is that it weakens the societies and threatens their existence. This problem is no doubt a prominent one in many primary societies in Kenya and raises the question of how commitment and involvement on the part of the members can be increased. Sometimes apathy is very evident in many primary societies and the managing committees are thereby given the whole responsibility of running such societies as they see fit. For any organization to exist and function successfully in a society, its organizational goals must have support from those whom it is serving and must also be adapted to the environment. The co-operatives are not exceptions to this rule and must seek support from the members by providing them with essential services and incorporating their requirements in their current goals. So far, there have been failures in this respect on the part of the managing committees, who must make a conscious effort to make their organizations both efficient and effective. On the subject of organizational goals and the environment, James D. Thompson and William J. McEwen have said that "the difference between effective and ineffective organizations may well lie in the initiative exercised by those in the organization who are responsible for goal-setting".[4]

In informal interviews in the Tetu Division of Nyeri District on the question of who should make decisions in society affairs, members responded by saying that it was the managing committees, for they knew what was good for the society better than the members did. In many cases, the committee members are not necessarily elected to the managing committees because of their knowledge of business management or dedication to the promotion of the co-operative movement, but because of their social standing in the community, for example, people in influential positions, such as traders, chiefs and teachers. Whether they have co-operative interests at heart does not even seem to matter much. In other words, the members of the managing committees of the rural co-operatives are predominantly the "rural bourgeoisie", usually in powerful positions which are equated with good co-operative leadership.

Another danger in this system of recruitment is that the committee members are elected to those positions in "political constituencies". Once a member is voted in, the practice has been for him to consider the interests of his "constituency", and not those of the whole society. This practice was well demonstrated in a case study of two co-operative societies in Kirinyaga district (it is also common in many societies), where a person who had mismanaged the affairs of the society was re-elected to the management committee.[5]

In places where co-operative societies cover a very wide geographical area and thereby create opportunities for farmers from many locations or divisions to belong to one or more co-operative societies, conflicts over which location or division should provide the chairman always arise. This point was well illustrated by the recent break-up of the Meru District Co-operative Union, because of claims that some areas were receiving more job allocations than others. This case also shows the significance of rotating power in various regions "as a way of maintaining an organizational equilibrium".[6] Sometimes society members complain that a chairman or other leader has been imposed on them, without their deciding or participating in the elections. Evidence from district co-operative unions and primary co-operative societies suggests that leadership conflicts and tensions are prominent features of the movement, and no remedial or corrective formula has been instituted up to the present time. This practice has inevitably affected the working relationships of the managing committees and the co-operative-society employees. In fact, many co-operative employees have decided to leave the movement because of such conflicts and also because the career prospects are not promising.

The end result has been that the movement has become inefficient and is handicapped in many ways. The immediate questions that should be answered within the movement have to do with efficiency—questions such as "When is a co-operative society efficient?" and "What criteria are most appropriate in measuring such efficiency?". The task of evaluating the co-operatives is a multi-faceted one, and various students of the movement have judged their success and failure by looking only at certain aspects and not at others. Raymond Apthorpe, for instance, has observed that to try to evaluate a complex set like co-operation is like trying to evaluate the Church.[7] The contemporary experience is that, to achieve management efficiency in an organization, pressure from below is an important catalyst. Looking at the present Kenyan co-operative societies in that light, we may say that management efficiency will not be achieved easily. In the first place, the membership, as I have already mentioned, is not wholeheartedly committed to the movement, and in most cases interest in co-operation is dying or dead, which renders the creation of pressure from below impossible.

In *Co-operatives and Rural Development in East Africa,* Carl Gösta Widstrand has touched on this most important aspect and has observed that:

> ... it is not until the members themselves feel a sense of involvement and ... have some control over the co-operative (through education, involvement in productive activities, etc.) that efficiency can be guaranteed by pressure from below, by active participation by the membership.[8]

The problem here is how to maximise the requisite active participation by the members and ultimately enable the movement to exert such pressure. One of the problems in this respect is that it is not unusual to find one farmer belonging to as many as four different co-operative societies at the same time. It would be a great burden for such a farmer to participate actively in all these single-purpose co-operative societies. Each such single-purpose co-operative, too, operates under its own managing committee, employs its own staff and is locally independent of any other co-operative society, except the district co-operative union, which functions as the "umbrella" of the primary societies in the district.

In attempts to create a situation in which close involvement of the members in their society affairs can be developed, various recommendations on how to set up farmers' marketing organizations have been made. David H. Pickard, writing on the factors affecting success and failure in farmers' co-operative associations, argues that "co-operation in agriculture must grow from the ground floor upwards and not be built from the penthouse downwards".[9] Perhaps the main objective of this organizational philosophy is to try to save the farmer from getting lost in big and complex co-operative institutions in the early stages of trying to make him change and adapt himself to new methods of farming. Pickard emphasizes this idea further by saying that

> ... the farmer responds to people he knows rather than to distant organizations or to abstract concepts. All this confirms ... the belief that the primary unit in agriculture must be small, local, utilising known and respected local leadership, so that the farmer may identify himself with this organization and think of it instinctively as "us" and not as "them".[10]

The spirit which the above quotation calls for on the part of the co-operative members is lacking in the primary societies in Kenya. This was confirmed in our co-operative case study, in which we found that the members regarded their society as an organization which they expected to distribute benefits to them, though they did not contribute their time and energy to its proper running.[11]

In trying to establish effective co-operative organisations and effective participation by the members, while bearing in mind the necessary conditions just discussed, it is important to determine the optimal size of a co-operative society. In this connection, there are two types of co-operative society that may be set up in a given area, that is, a multi-purpose society or a single-purpose society. One may have certain advantages over the other, as will be discussed shortly. However, the trend in Kenya, as stated in the recent Sessional Paper, points to the multi-purpose type of co-operative society. The paper states that:

> At the village level, the policy is one of developing viable primaries on a multi-commodity, multi-purpose pattern, so that the one village society may, in the long run, meet all the economic needs of its members.[12]

One of the advantages of a multi-purpose co-operative society, if appropriately located, is that a farmer belongs to only one co-operative society, to which he or she takes the agricultural produce for marketing. Such a co-operative society would attract the majority of farmers, especially where they market more than one commodity through the co-operative societies. The location of any co-operative society is of great importance to farmers. It should be nearby, since many farmers in the rural areas have to walk long distances to attend society meetings, to deliver their produce and also to get their farming supplies, such as cattle and pig feeds, fertilisers and so on. The geographical area covered by the co-operative society is of importance too, for, as we saw earlier on, society members often complain that leaders whom they did not know before have been imposed on them to run their societies. It may be argued that, if the geographical unit of a co-operative society is small enough, the members will be in a position to elect as their leaders people they trust and know well. The significance of this fact is that for a long time now effective leadership has been one of the scarcest resources in the movement, is critically short in some places and must be cultivated if successful co-operative societies are to thrive in the country.

Also the members' feeling of "belonging" must be cultivated, in order to close the existing gap between the members and the leaders. In this respect, the understanding of the psychology of the rural farmers (an aspect that has been neglected so far) is of vital importance. In informal interviews, rural farmers who are members of fairly large co-operatives always indicate their distrust or fear or both of being told to contribute money either for investing in a building or in some sort of machinery that is at a considerable distance from them. This practice by the co-operative leaders is very evident today, and has certainly caused considerable confusion and anxiety to the members. In some cases, the major source of the farmers' suspicions is the fact that leaders come from far off and are not to be trusted with money for such investments. It has been argued that, by having co-operative societies of reasonable size, such attitudes could be mitigated considerably. J. A. E. Morley has pointed out that:

> ... small co-operatives account for a more intimate relationship between the members and the co-operative than is possible in large organizations, the fruits of which are a greater willingness to accept discipline, since this is self-imposed, and a greater willingness to subscribe capital, since the advantages of doing so are more direct and immediately apparent.[13]

Let us now turn to this important aspect of the appropriate size for a co-operative that can be established in rural areas, with the aim of cultivating that intimate relationship between the members and the society. The co-operative societies in Kenya have hitherto been either multi-purpose co-operatives or single-purpose co-operatives. However, there has been some development in the direction of recommending one kind in some areas of the country and the other in other areas, depending on the circumstances and the environmental conditions under which they are to function.

The new Co-operative Societies Act gives the Commissioner for Co-operatives considerable powers to enable him to guide the co-operative movement in a new direction. One of these powers is that he can insist that small mono-crop or single-purpose societies shall amalgamate to form sufficiently viable multi-purpose units, perhaps affiliated to a co-operative union. By so doing, he will ensure that each society is sufficiently large to be able to justify its employing the staff necessary to perform its basic functions effectively, while certain services, such as the provision of transport or buying and selling in bulk can be performed by the co-operative union.[14] These measures were promulgated because of the dangerous situation which the movement got into during the post-independence period, when many co-operative societies were formed, for the most part by politicians as part of the *harambee* effort in their constituencies. In most cases, no planning was done for them and consequently they had to face many organizational difficulties later.

At the moment, the Government is greatly encouraging the strengthening of the present co-operative societies to make them into more viable organizations. Göran Hyden has pointed out that "in Kenya, the effort is to consolidate already existing marketing co-operatives and turn them into multi-purpose institutions, offering a wider range of services to the members".[15] While this move has received support within the movement, single-purpose co-operatives have gained some support in some quarters within the movement as well. However, the latter are considered to be not as conducive to bringing the farmers together to the same extent as the former, which, as G. Solomon also argues, "if properly organized, will in no way weaken the efficiency of each individual sector of the co-operative, (but) will, through its enlarged activity, increase its economic power".[16]

It is now time to try to weigh the advantages and the disadvantages of multi-purpose and single-purpose societies, since this will be the main point of the case study that follows.

The amalgamation of co-operative societies of either kind has been a question frequently discussed in the contemporary co-operative movement. The effort to try to find the most appropriate pattern to be followed is partly because of the present demands for consolidating the existing societies and thereby giving them a more forward-looking direction than has been the case in the past. The following points can be put forward in favour of multi-purpose co-operative societies.

(*a*) As more than one function is delegated to the co-operative society, the relationship between the farmer and the society reaches a higher level of integration and therefore forms a stronger bond.

(*b*) The farmer has to raise less capital for his share contribution. Instead of contributing to several societies, he has to buy only one share in a multi-purpose society.

(*c*) The co-operative potentials with regard to leadership, enthusiasm, etc., in a village are not split but are concentrated in one society.

(*d*) There is usually a reduction in the cost per unit produced or turned over, as administrative costs will be reduced by being spread over several activities.

(*e*) Often, only the formation of multi-purpose societies can increase the viability of co-operative activities which otherwise could not be carried out. The business volume of one activity may not be large enough to form an economic basis for the operation of a society.[17]

The disadvantages of multi-purpose societies (single-purpose advantages) can be stated as follows:

(*a*) The burden put on the management is considerably heavier than in the single-purpose society, and with increasing size there is the danger that proper control and supervision of the society may be lost.

(*b*) An all-round manager for this type of job is usually hard to find.

(*b*) The dispersal of effort often leads to the neglect of certain activities, especially for extension work.

(*d*) The exact costs of certain operations are hard to assess, owing to the difficulties of correctly allocating the overhead expenses.

(*e*) Conflicting interests may arise within the membership.

In amalgamating various kinds of co-operative societies into any of the two categories already referred to, it is very important that the advantages and disadvantages of each category are discussed thoroughly and explained to the members.

The experience of the movement so far has been that the leaders only sell the ideas that they have already decided among themselves, without first seeking the opinions of their clientele. In effect, they only request them at general meetings to approve their preferences. The economic aspects should certainly be considered as well as the sociological aspects, for irrational motives, such as one area having reached a cer-

Table 1. *Population Size and Land Area by Locations in Northern Tetu.*

Location	Population	Area, km²
Aguthi	28 794	82
Thigingi	28 070	67
Muhoya	16 417	44
Tetu	18 932	49
Total	92 213	242

Source: *Kenya Population Census*, 1969.

tain level of development, or traditional hostility between two neighbouring or distant villages or locations may be issues of considerable difficuly in amalgamating two or more co-operative societies belonging to such villages or locations. To examine the nature and intensity of such issues, I present the following case study of some co-operative societies in Tetu Division, Nyeri District, where the amalgamation of 14 societies was recommended and accepted by the primary-society leaders and the members in principle but not in fact.

The Attitudes of the Co-operative Members in Tetu Division to the Proposed Amalgamation

Tetu Division is one of the six divisions in Nyeri District; it is located just on the southern part of the saddle between Mount Kenya and the Aberdares. Its altitude is between 5 000 and 7 000 feet above sea-level and it has an area of 85 square miles. On the western side of the division is the Aberdare range, which rises to well over 13 000 feet above sea-level, whereas on the north is the territory between the Aberdares and the Nyeri township. On the eastern side is the Sagana River and on the southern side the Gura River. The Division covers four administrative locations and has a total population of 92 213 people (see Table 1).

Tetu Division serves as the transportation route from Nairobi to the north-west. However, the road and railway is just east of the Division and consequently any industrialization would be external to the Division, possibly at Kiganjo or Karatina. Due to the different ecological zones, Tetu is a mixed-farming area, and dairy production is one of the most important monetary activities in the Division. The completion of land consolidation and registration during the mid-1950s has made the extensive utilization of the land possible and in fact has facilitated the extension of cash crops. Also of much importance in rural development, in addition to the favourable ecological conditions, is the fact that the inhabitants in the area have all along responded very readily to innovative agricultural methods. The four dairy societies in Tetu were among the first to be started in Kenya in the early 1940s.

At present there are 14 agricultural marketing co-operatives, covering every part of the Division. These co-operatives have been functioning at different levels in the four locations and within the Division as well. For example, all the coffee farmers in the Division belong to the only coffee co-operative for the whole Division. Muhoya location has one dairy and one pig co-operative and shares a pyrethrum co-operative with Tetu location. Tetu location has two dairy co-operatives and one pig co-operative. Thigingi location has two pyrethrum co-operatives, one pig co-operative (it shares a second one with Aguthi location) and one dairy co-operative (it shares a second one with the same location). Finally, Aguthi location has one pig co-operative. The state of the co-operatives in the Division then is that each location has certain specific co-operatives operating within its geographical boundaries, whereas it shares another kind of co-operative with the neighbouring location, with the exception of the coffee co-operative, which functions as a single-purpose co-operative for the whole Division. All these co-operatives are (in accordance with the Co-operatives Act) members of the Nyeri District Co-operative Union (see Table 2).

The disintegrative nature of the co-operatives in Tetu forced many farmers in the area to belong to more than one society. A good number belong to as many as four co-operatives simultaneously. Each co-operative society has its managing committee of nine people (in accordance with the Act), who are elected by the members and who draw an allowance of Ksh. 10

Table 2. *Types of Co-operative Societies, Membership and Turnover in K£ in the end of 1968.*

Type of co-operative	Number	Membership	Turnover, K£
Dairy	5	2 239	68 789
Pigs	5	3 340	85 938
Pyrethrum	3	2 066	25 564
Coffee	1	5 652	37 412
Total	14	13 297	317 703

for each meeting. The recommended number of meetings is one every 3 months or one every month, but in most cases the committees meet more often than that. Altogether there are 126 managing-committee members. Each dairy society runs its own vehicle for milk delivery to Nyeri township. The employees of co-operatives such as these are usually of two categories. The first category is that of graded staff, who are employed by the district co-operative unions and seconded to the primary societies. The second category is that of the ungraded staff employed by individual primary societies. Tetu Coffee-growers Co-operative Society, which is the only single-purpose co-operative, operates its own lorries for transporting coffee, while the pig co-operatives rent union vehicles for transporting pigs to the railway station at Kiganjo.

In considering ways and means of reducing the number of these societies, the Nyeri District Co-operative Union decided that this could be achieved by amalgamating the existing co-operatives along the lines of single-purpose co-operative societies in each division and thereby reducing the number to only four. The amalgamation decision was not, however, reached in a vacuum or without justifiable reasoning. It was based on an economic feasibility study that indicated that, by implementing the recommendations, an effort would have been made to reduce the overhead costs, so as to ensure the maximum return to the farmers.

Thus, in amalgamating all the five dairy societies to form one divisional single-purpose society, transportation would be centralized and proper control from one point would eliminate the misuse of vehicles. The pig societies, if merged, would ensure a more viable co-operative, and so would the pyrethrum co-operatives. The whole idea was to re-organize them on similar lines to the coffee society in the Division. The rationale in the whole process took account of economic considerations and nothing else. So far, the views or opinions of the co-operative members were not known, nor were they sought with regard to the proposed amalgamation of their societies. This is an important principle, if we regard the members as the backbone of the movement; they should be involved in the decision-making on matters affecting their organizations. In fact, without the members there would be no such thing as co-operatives, nor would there be the managing committees which direct the affairs of these institutions on behalf of the members who elected them. In such circumstances, co-operative members have a right to be consulted on major decisions. The major aim of this study is therefore to examine the opinions or views of the members of the co-operative societies in Tetu Division regarding the proposed amalgamation on the single-purpose pattern.

An attempt will be made to examine the extent to which the members' views were sought and the reasons that led some committee members to favour one form of amalgamation and not the other. Co-operative members, like those in *harambee* groups, must be given much more responsibility and must be made to feel that they have something at stake. This seems to be a very important field of research that has not received the same attention as other aspects of the movement. In considering both of these rural institutions, Göran Hyden has observed that "self-help groups established to produce public amenities easily gain support in the local communities, while marketing co-operatives do not".[18] If they are to be as successful as these self-help groups, they must cultivate a new outlook. In the proposed amalgamation, few assumptions could be made with regard to the responses of the society members. The first assumption was that the majority of the members would prefer some type of amalgamation which would lessen the burden laid on farmers by belonging to several different co-operative societies. The second assumption was that the more prosperous and well-to-do cooperative societies, with clear-cut goals and objectives for the future, would not favour merging with the poor ones, which lacked anything to show as an example of success in the past. In other words, the past history of the societies and the area where they were located would play an important role in amalgamation. In fact, there were many assumptions that could have been made, but these seemed to be the most relevant and influenced the decision of each person in determining whether to amalgamate and with whom on single-purpose lines outside the location, as recommended, or whether to amalgamate along multi-purpose lines within the location.

The sample consisted of 332 respondents (242 men and 90 women). We used a random-sampling method on the land-registration rolls, by picking every 31st name in the register. Of the total sample, 254 respondents were currently active co-operative members. Some of the remaining 78 respondents had ceased to be co-operators, either because they had discontinued producing anything to be marketed through the societies or because their cows were dry. Some, of course, had never been co-operative members.

A. Favourableness to Amalgamation

The first set of questions asked was aimed at finding out from the co-operative members themselves whether the existing number of co-operatives in their division presented inconveniences to their farming activities, in the sense that they had to belong to more than one, which meant attending so many different meetings, walking long distances to the places where such meetings were to be held, and having to pay for so many shares. The objective was to weigh the members' opinions as to whether they favoured or disfavoured amalgamation of their societies, regardless of the specific kind. The responses were analysed according to the four locations in the Division, and also according to the progressiveness of the farmers interviewed. Progressive farmers are those who adopt new agricultural ideas, such as cash crops, graded cows, and similar farming innovations earlier than their fellow farmers. Therefore the most progressive farmers are the *first adopters* of inno-

Table 3. *Location and Progressiveness by Attitude toward Amalgamation.*

Q. Do you favour or disfavour amalgamation of co-ops.?	Location				Progressiveness				Division
Attitude	Thigingi %	Aguthi %	Tetu %	Muhoya %	Most prog. %	Upper middle %	Lower middle %	Laggards %	Total %
Favours	90	89	87	81	94	86	88	77	86
Disfavours	3	4	6	16	3	11	8	3	7
No opinion	7	7	7	3	3	3	4	20	7
Total	100	100	100	100	100	100	100	100	
Base	113	106	76	37	88	91	93	60	332

vations, followed by the majority of adopters (upper middle and lower middle), and finally the laggards who have not adopted anything yet.

The farmers' attitudes towards the amalgamation of the co-operative societies were highly favourable (see Table 3). Almost 9 out of every 10 farmers in Tetu Division favoured amalgamation. More of the most progressive farmers favoured amalgamation than the less progressive farmers. The explanation of this is that the most progressive farmers were the ones who really experienced the inconveniences of having to belong to many co-operative societies and other marketing organizations like the KTDA, since they had various agricultural commodities to channel through the respective co-operatives. Such a progressive farmer in Tetu, for example, is very likely to have coffee, graded cattle, pigs, pyrethrum, tea and macadamia trees. So a reduced number of co-operative societies would allow them more time to dedicate to other activities. They also had an economic reason for favouring amalgamation. The bargaining power of small co-operative societies is weak, especially when negotiating with the district co-operative unions and other marketing organizations. Moreover increased payments may accrue from reduced costs. Perhaps another

Table 4. *Location and Progressiveness by Type of Amalgamation Preferred.*

Q. What type of amalgamation do you prefer—single-purpose divisional or multi-purpose locational co-ops.?	Location				Progressiveness				Division
Amalgamation type	Thigingi %	Aguthi %	Tetu %	Muhoya %	Most prog. %	Upper middle %	Lower middle %	Laggards %	Total %
Single-purpose	50	69	53	27	52	55	59	47	54
Multi-purpose	37	21	41	65	39	36	36	31	36
No opinion	13	10	6	8	9	9	5	22	10
Total	100	100	100	100	100	100	100	100	100
Base	113	106	76	37	88	91	93	60	332

important reason was that most of the progressive farmers in Tetu and in the country as a whole are the chairmen and committee members of the co-operative societies,[19] and therefore amalgamation would in effect strengthen and elevate the status of the societies. Their leadership roles would be enhanced, too, and gain them higher social status in the community. The least progressive farmers could not care less, since they do not have much at stake; as many as 20% did not express an opinion either way. Some of the farmers in this category were not co-operative members and were unaware of the existence of the 14 co-operatives in the area.

As regards the sex distribution, 88% of the men and 82% of the women favoured amalgamation. The great interest in amalgamation shown by both sexes is an indication that women are just as active in society affairs as men. In fact, they literally shoulder the great burden of having to deliver their produce over long distances on their backs. Education and literacy differences among the interviewees seem to have had no great significance in deciding either way. There was no great difference in the replies between respondents from small families (households of up to 8 members) and large families (households of 9 or more members).

B. Type of Amalgamation

The idea of having either single-purpose divisional co-operatives or multi-purpose locational co-operatives had been a subject of discussion in the area in the top leadership circles, but only to a very limited extent among the members. It seemed important to check the kind of co-operative amalgamation that the members felt could give them better service. The nature of the two kinds of co-operatives referred to above were mentioned and explained to the respondents.

This question seems to be crucial for the future policies of these co-operatives and the responses portray a distinct polarization across locational boundaries (see Table 4). The respondents from three neighbouring locations—Thigingi, Aguthi, and Tetu—predominantly chose single-purpose divisional co-operatives, while those in Muhoya location strongly favoured multi-purpose locational co-operatives. There may be many explanations of these responses, but first let us consider the ecological factors in the four locations.

More than half of Muhoya location, which borders on the Aberdare forest, is situated within the high bracken zone, where the annual rainfall is plentiful and allows of good yields from cash crops such as tea, pyrethrum, and wheat. Dairy cattle and sheep, which are *high-income earners,* do very well. Subsistence crops, such as vegetables and potatoes, also do well. Small parts of the Tetu and Thigingi locations are in this fertile zone too, while the rest, plus more than half of Aguthi location, is in the Kikuyu grass zone, where coffee, dairy cattle and sheep are the income earners, and potatoes and vegetables are the subsistence food crops. Finally, a good part of Aguthi location is in the star-grass zone, where only coffee and dairy cattle are the main income earners and the yields of food crops are poor. The rainfall in the three latter locations is less than 40 inches annually, which is somewhat lower than in Muhoya location, and is inevitably a controlling factor in agricultural development.

Owing to the favourable ecological conditions, plus the capacity and readiness of the people in Muhoya location to absorb innovative agricultural methods, and particularly graded dairy cattle, the location has always forged ahead in all spheres of agricultural development. Historically, the location has been the pioneer of co-operative societies, and particularly dairy co-operatives, since the early 1940s. The late Senior Chief Muhoya was responsible for cultivating this capacity for rapid change in the farmers in the area, and today one hardly finds any non-graded cattle in the area, whereas in Aguthi such willingness to change is not evident to any appreciable extent. These factors have boosted farming activities in Muhoya location and consequently the farmers receive steady incomes, unlike those in other locations and particularly Aguthi.

Another very important explanation of why the Muhoya farmers favoured a multi-purpose co-operative society in their location may be that their co-operatives are better organized and have clear-cut development goals and objectives, which are lacking in other societies in the area. For example, the dairy co-operative society in the area recently constructed a big modern building to house the society's offices, dairy, board-room, stores and three shops for renting. Beside the building, a petrol station has been installed and the society has already successfully attracted all the motorists in the area to get their petrol supplies from there. Only one other dairy society in the area has an office.

Confidence in the leadership is very important in the co-operative movement and where leaders have been trusted and are faithful, the members try to keep them as long as possible. Eventually, such leaders use that trust to get higher offices in the nation. In this respect, the farmers in Muhoya location were reluctant to risk the chance of losing their present leaders. They also pointed out that their present advanced stage of development was due to the co-operation within the location; to continue operating in that spirit, what they needed was self-determination and local autonomy in their location. The recent appearance in a national television broadcast of some *harambee* groups from the area who were constructing a cattle dip was frequently referred to as an illustration of what they meant by locational unity in all their development activities. Another advantage that some societies in the location (dairy cattle and pigs) have is that they are closer to Nyeri township than the other societies and it is anticipated that a tarmac road will reach the society headquarters soon.

This behaviour of co-operatives, displayed in the responses of the members, is an important phenomenon, in the sense that, despite the fact that their common objective should be to join together and fight the middleman, it seems that they have developed some parochial attitudes. In other words, one of the reasons for the proposed amalgamation was to strengthen the movement in the Division, but for some co-operative societies there was the additional issue of who should amalgamate with whom. The rich ones do not want to associate with the poor ones, while the poor ones do not hesitate to amalgamate with the rich ones. The Aguthi co-operatives, which are relatively poor, strongly supported the single-purpose divisional co-operatives, which would have provided an opportunity to join hands with those in Muhoya location. This attitude was supported by the Tetu co-operatives (41 %), which came closer to the Muhoya position.

The least progressive farmers favoured single-purpose divisional co-operatives more than multi-purpose locational co-operatives. The reason may have been that they realized that there was a prospective gain from increased membership on the divisional level. The majority of such farmers are in both the Aguthi and the Thigingi locations and their responses demonstrated the solidarity of this category of farmers in an attempt to share the co-operative benefits with the wealthy ones. Again, those who did not express preferences for one type over the other (22 %) were the least progressive farmers.

As regards the sex breakdown, 57 % of the men and 47 % of the women preferred single-purpose divisional co-operatives. The difference does not seem to be very significant, but the men seemed to prefer enlarged societies outside their locational boundaries. Today this is important, especially on the part of the leaders, who may be seeking high offices in the district or in the country, since large co-operatives today provide an important platform for any kind of campaign outside the loca-

Table 5. *Education and Literacy by Type of Amalgamation.*

Q. What type of amalgamation do you prefer — single-purpose divisional or multi-purpose locational co-ops.?	Education			Literacy				Division
Type of amalgamation	None %	Up to 3 yrs. %	4 yrs. %	None %	Vernacular %	Swahili %	English %	Total %
Single-purpose	53	53	57	52	50	62	54	54
Multi-purpose	34	37	37	35	41	29	41	36
No opinion	13	10	6	13	9	9	5	10
Total	100	100	100	100	100	100	100	100
Base	137	100	95	134	66	76	56	332

tional boundaries. Also it may well be that men are generally better informed about the outside world than women, a factor that may have influenced their desire for a divisional outlook on society amalgamation on a wider geographical level.

However, 42 % of the women and 33 % of the men preferred multi-purpose locational co-operatives. The major explanation of this difference is that in many areas of the country more women than men participate in almost all the activities of the co-operative societies. At general meetings, and any other special meetings, most often they are the main attenders. It is mostly they who participate in any kind of communal work called for by the societies. Their husbands are usually away from home and they are therefore left in charge and are responsible for the welfare of the entire family. At informal interviews, they pointed out that, with locational co-operatives, the long journeys on foot to such co-operative activities could be shortened. Their opportunities of attending co-operative meetings regularly would be increased too. Because of these circumstances, they argued that co-operatives should be established at suitable geographical points.

Table 6. *Location and Progressiveness by Disposition of Committees under Single-purpose Divisional Co-operatives.*

Q. What should happen to the committees of the co-ops. that amalgamate to form single-purpose divisional co-ops.?	Location				Progressiveness				Division
Disposition of committees	Thigingi %	Aguthi %	Tetu %	Muhoya %	Most progs. %	Upper middle %	Lower middle %	Laggards %	Total %
Continue to exist	10	14	17	35	11	25	16	10	16
Form one committee	73	76	74	46	78	64	74	62	70
No opinion	17	10	9	19	11	11	10	28	14
Total	100	100	100	100	100	100	100	100	100
Base	113	106	76	37	88	91	93	60	332

No significant differences between people with different levels of education and literacy were found in terms of their attitudes to the type of amalgamation (see Table 5). This phenomenon can be attributed to the numerous appeals in the country for closer co-operation and unity in the development efforts. The radio and newspapers such as *Taifaleo,* which is widely read in the rural areas, have been disseminating information with the same content. The differences in attitudes between the small family and the large family were not very significant.

By amalgamating the existing 13 co-operative societies (pigs, dairy cattle and pyrethrum) into single-purpose divisional co-operatives, according to the economic feasibility study that had been carried out, the Nyeri District Co-operative Union planned to have only three managing committees instead of the existing 13 managing committees. This was a measure aimed at considerably reducing the committees' sitting allow-

Table 7. *Sex, Education and Literacy by Disposition of Committees under Single-purpose Divisional Co-operatives.*

Q. What should happen to the committees of the co-ops. that amalgamate to form one single-purpose divisional co-op.?	Sex		Education			Literacy				Division
Disposition of committees	Male %	Female %	None %	Up to 3 yrs. %	4 yrs. or more %	None %	Vern. %	Swah. %	Eng. %	Total %
Continue to exist	15	19	20	19	8	20	21	11	9	16
Form one committee	71	65	65	65	81	63	62	79	80	70
Don't know/No opinion	13	16	15	16	10	17	17	10	9	13
Other	1	—	—	—	1	—	—	—	2	1
Total	100	100	100	100	100	100	100	100	100	100
Base	242	90	137	100	95	134	66	76	56	332

ances, which were already costing the farmers substantial amounts of money. The implementation of that proposal, it was argued, would save the societies money which could be diverted to increasing farmers' payments. However, this would have depended on the willingness of such societies to disband the old managing committees. Assuming that the amalgamation was to materialize, the question of whether to form only *one* new committee or to let the old ones continue functioning was put to the society members.

Table 6 shows that Muhoya location differs markedly from the rest. It seems that the societies there are not as much opposed to continuing with the old committees as others in the division. As I mentioned earlier on, the co-operative societies there have achieved more progress, compared with the rest, and therefore the members seemed somewhat uncertain as to whether to remove the old committees or not. The case in Aguthi location is the opposite, for there is nothing that the

Table 8. *Location and Progressiveness by Disposition of Committees under Multi-purpose Locational Co-operatives.*

Q. What should happen to the committees of the co-ops. that amalgamate to form multi-purpose locational co-ops.?	Location				Progressiveness				
Disposition of committees	Thigingi %	Aguthi %	Tetu %	Muhoya %	Most progs. %	Upper middle %	Lower middle %	Laggards %	Total %
Continue to exist	10	13	12	32	9	21	14	13	16
Form one committee	73	76	79	49	81	64	76	62	70
No opinion	17	11	9	19	10	15	10	25	14
Total	100	100	100	100	100	100	100	100	100
Base	113	106	76	37	88	91	93	60	332

society members can point to to indicate the committee's achievements in the past, something that compels them to seek new leadership on the divisional level. Thigingi and Tetu locations are not far from this situation either.

However, it could be safely concluded that the people of the four locations thought that there were some economic benefits to be gained by reducing the expenditure on the committees' sitting allowances. It seems that this was a relatively less complicated economic issue to justify the proposed amalgamation or the multi-purpose kind preferred by Muhoya location. Slight differences on the same issue were shown between those with 3 and those with 4 or more years of education.

Table 7 shows that the higher the level of education, the greater was the preference for eliminating the old committees and replacing them with one new committee. More support for forming only one committee came from those who had 4 or more years of education. Also there was concern about the

Table 9. *Sex, Education and Literacy by Disposition of Committees under Multi-purpose Locational Co-operatives.*

Q. What should happen to the committees of the co-ops. that amalgamate to form multi-purpose locational co-ops.?	Sex		Education			Literacy				
Disposition of committees	Male %	Female %	None %	Up to 3 yrs. %	4 yrs. or more %	None %	Vern. %	Swahili %	Eng. %	Total %
Continue to exist	14	17	18	17	6	18	20	8	7	16
Form one committee	72	69	67	65	84	66	60	81	84	70
Don't know/No opinion	14	14	15	18	10	16	20	11	9	14
Total	100	100	100	100	100	100	100	100	100	100
Base	242	90	137	100	95	134	66	76	56	332

existence of so many committees among those who had no education, for example, 65% wished to have only one committee and only 20% wanted the present committees to continue functioning. Only very slight differences were found in terms of literacy and family, as regarded the opinion about the disposition of committees under single-purpose divisional amalgamation.

The same question was asked, but this time about the multi-purpose societies. The purpose of this was to try to determine to what extent the members wanted to eliminate the old committees on every structural society level, i.e. on the divisional and locational levels. The question was: Suppose, for the moment, that most people favour multi-purpose locational co-operatives; what should happen to the committees of societies which amalgamate to form one multi-purpose co-operative? Should they continue to exist as sub-committees or should one new committee replace them all?

About the same preference pattern is repeated here as for the single-purpose divisional co-operatives (Table 8). We may now conclude that the members' views on the disposition of the many existing committees after amalgamation is very uniform—that only one committee should be formed. The Muhoya location shows unwillingness, relative to other locations on the question, to do away with the already existing committees straight away.

Table 9 shows little difference from Table 7. Finally, we may come to the definite conclusion that the majority of the society members prefer only one managing committee for each co-operative society, whether multi-purpose or single-purpose, as recommended in the amalgamation proposal.

Discussion and Conclusion

The process of amalgamating co-operative societies into larger economic and social units is a complex and difficult one, in the sense that members of such co-operatives and their managing committees will not necessarily follow the amalgamation recommendations made by the co-operative officials. The present case study shows that there are other factors that members worry about than the economic ones. The comment has already been made that in developing areas co-operatives are more than economic institutions, in the sense that they are also social institutions which provide other essential services. Against this background, in amalgamating co-operative societies, it is important that careful consideration should be given to the issues in terms of advantages and disadvantages. Such consideration should not be concentrated only on the economic factors but also on the equally important sociological factors. This is because such amalgamation involves the re-organisation of people's attitudes and their traditional ways of carrying on their daily co-operative activities. If an amalgamation is carried out because it would look tidy on the chart of the co-operative movement, such a merger will not go very far. Such a type of amalgamation only causes unrest among the members and the committees and also destroys the much-needed co-operative spirit.

This underlines the importance of involving the co-operative members in making the decision whether to amalgamate or not, and on the type of amalgamation to be preferred. The implication of this strategy is that in this way the members are placed in a crucial position and will identify and support the objectives of such societies once they have amalgamated. In seeking approval or support for a planned amalgamation, it is important that not only the advantages but also the disadvantages of such a move should be thoroughly explained to the members and their committees. The movement has been very weak on this point, as was not surprisingly noted in the Tetu co-operatives. Usually, the emphasis is put on the advantages of amalgamation in one way, but the disadvantages are deliberately never mentioned. In other words, the co-operatives are left with no alternative but to go along with the amalgamation plans. However, in societies where the managing committees have co-operative interests at heart, they usually indicate what they prefer, depending on what they want to achieve for their members. This spirit was displayed by the co-operative societies in Muhoya location in this study and confirmed the second assumption that the very active co-operatives with clear-cut goals and objectives would be reluctant to join with the less well-off co-operatives.

The importance of this stand taken by the Muhoya co-operatives to the proposal to amalgamate to form a multi-purpose society within the location is that it reveals the development or emergence of the self-reliance now being cultivated by the co-operatives in the handling of their affairs and particularly in deploying their resources and energies to develop their community. This can be interpreted as a departure from the traditional functions of the co-operatives of just distributing financial benefits to the farmers. This also implies that these co-operatives in Muhoya location have reached a position of security, to the extent that their objectives are wholeheartedly accepted by the inhabitants of the location. As our data indicate, the members here seem reluctant to throw out the old committees, an indication that their work has satisfied their clientele. This is very important for the organizational survival, an element that is lacking in many co-operatives in the country, including many in the other three locations of the Division.

It may be argued that, with the present self-conscious effort to join together in a multi-purpose pattern, members will now have a wider ground for participation in the affairs of their society, in line with the philosophy that "co-operatives could provide a ground within which the peasant can develop a feeling for the operation of a democracy and a sense of participation in his own growth and development, while giving him some sense of security through group association".[20] This form of co-operation would probably go a long way towards eliminating many of the weaknesses of the movement today, namely, disloyalty, apathy and non-involvement on the part of the members. Members would have an opportunity of scrutinising the work of the managing committees and that of the staff. Such an arrangement would also offer the members a better chance of electing leaders whom they really know and trust. The objectives sought by the proposed amalgamation could also be achieved by this form of amalgamation.

In the movement today, the most important issue is, what is the most suitable geographical area for a given co-operative to cover? A senior co-operative official recently put the issue in this way: "Today the major problem facing the co-operative movement is the geographical units that co-operatives should take, to make the members more active, concerned and interested in their society affairs, so as not to feel that these are just organizations imposed on them by the government." The concern here is that mentioned earlier—attempting to make the members develop the feeling of being "insiders" rather than "outsiders" vis-à-vis their societies.

While multi-purpose societies need an extremely capable and experienced manager, single-purpose societies would not be terribly demanding in terms of management capability, since they handle only one type of commodity. To what extent this form of co-operation would maximise individual participation and involvement in the society affairs, however, is not clear.

The optimal size of a co-operative society is that which is capable of maximising the members' participation. As in any other rural institution, effective participation becomes less where the organization covers a large area and where the membership is very large. Provided the operational costs are not unwarranted, the smaller the co-operative, the greater the chances of its being effective in the community and the greater its capability in manipulating its environment. This supports the view that "effective organization and effective participation are governed by the rule of optimal size".[21] Where the size encourages the members to take an interest in the society affairs and where the management realizes the implication of this, the society will probably have a chance of being efficient; otherwise, members will become critical of it. This has been a great failure in the co-operative movement; members are not critical enough of the managing committees, which causes them to deteriorate.

In concluding, certain points which have come out of this study should be emphasised with regard to the process of amalgamating existing co-operative societies. First, amalgamation should not be imposed upon the co-operative societies, for this, more than anything else, would endanger the co-operative spirit. Secondly, in the whole process, a multi-disciplinary approach should be utilized in trying to understand the whole historical development of such societies and also the area in which they are situated. Thirdly, both the advantages and disadvantages of either single-purpose or multi-purpose co-operatives should be fully explained to the members, who should be given the opportunity to participate in making the decision as to the type of amalgamation they would like to have.

J. L. Murungi

The Co-operative Movement in Kenya

The philosophy which guides co-operation in Kenya does not differ from that of the Rochdale Pioneers in 19th-century England. It is based on self-reliance, self-sufficiency, and service to and promotion of the members' interests through a voluntary movement, in which the noble ideals of equality, economic and social justice, and democracy are upheld. The ultimate objectives of the movement are to change the prevailing economic and social order and to eliminate exploitation, actions which are prerequisite to the achievement of economic and social justice.

Historical Background

The co-operative movement in Kenya was started by European farmers as early as 1908 for the purpose of marketing their cereal crops, fruits and dairy products. This early movement in Kenya, it must be noted, was not quite in the spirit of the Rochdale Pioneers, in that it did not observe the principle of open membership.

It was not until the mid-1940's that the British Government agreed to introduce co-operation in the African colonies as a piecemeal programme for the development of the African land units of that time. Consequently, Kenya enacted the Co-operative Ordinance in 1945, which was followed by the creation, in 1946, of a department under a Registrar of Co-operatives,

J. L. Murungi is Acting Assistant Commissioner for Co-operative Development in the Ministry of Co-operatives and Social Services, Nairobi.

whose objective was to promote farm-produce-marketing co-operatives in the African land units. Thereafter, approximately 200 co-operative societies were registered to market farm produce, generally cereals and also some poultry products.

The newly formed co-operatives had no economic basis, in that they were dealing with the subsistence type of produce. However, as the years went by and in the wake of African nationalism in Kenya in the late 1940's and early 1950's, the colonial government was compelled by circumstances to allow Africans to grow some cash crops, though under very strict controls.

With the planting of cash crops, such as coffee and pyrethrum, by small-scale African growers, who were scattered all over the producing areas, there was no alternative for the government but to allow the formation of co-operatives as a matter of necessity for processing and marketing purposes. It must be pointed out here that membership of the newly formed co-operatives was compulsory, since no planting licences were issued to non-members.

With land consolidation in the mid-1950s, the efficiency of production was increased, due to several factors, among the most important of which were the availability of credit to African small-holders holding title deeds for their consolidated units and the fact that farms (small-holdings) could be better planned and consequently better utilized as single units. As a result of consolidation, many more cash crops were grown and expansion in the planting of coffee and pyrethrum continued with minimum hindrances. The country was becoming politically mature fairly fast and development had to be speeded up for the *Wananchi* (citizens). Co-operatives were the best instrument for facilitating the socio-economic transfiguration of the rural areas just prior to and during the transition period.

Up to the year of Kenya's independence (1963), co-operatives were regarded merely as vehicles for introducing limited cash crops to the African small-holders. With independence, however, the picture changed and many new types of co-operatives were formed. There appeared, for the first time, numerous multi-purpose co-operatives, farm-purchase co-operatives, which were formed for the acquisition of the large farms previously owned by foreigners, and many other special types of co-operatives. No doubt quite a number of them were formed haphazardly and without the necessary consideration of the "felt economic need" for the formation. As a result, many of the newly formed co-operatives did not go far before they disintegrated and went into liquidation, in accordance with the provisions of the Co-operative Act. In a number of them, the management was inadequate, records were not kept, funds were misappropriated, members withdrew their support and inevitably many of the remaining members became disloyal.

All this resulted in an ugly picture being painted of the movement at large. There was condemnation for the movement from those who were adversely affected by the loss of their share capital or other contributions as a result of the failures. At the end of 1969, there were 1443 co-operative societies in the Commissioner's Register, of which only 56% (802 co-operatives) were estimated to be active. The active co-operatives have an annual turnover of over K£ 20 million, which benefits about three-quarters of a million members.

As it was aware that rural development and the proper distribution of the country's wealth could only be effectively achieved through the co-operative movement, the Kenya Government took certain specific measures to improve the effectiveness and efficiency of the co-operatives. These measures have been dealt with at length in the Second National Development Plan (1970–74) and more specifically in the Co-operative Development Policy for Kenya in the Government's Sessional Paper No. 8 of 1970. Earlier on, the Government introduced the new Co-operative Societies Act of 1966 (revised in 1967) and also the Co-operative Societies Rules of 1969, which gave the Commissioner for Co-operative Development wide powers to prevent misappropriation and misuse of funds, and also empowered him to act as he saw fit to improve the overall efficiency of the co-operative movement. The Commissioner, under these powers, may take action to remove management committees and to replace them with his own appointed committees for a limited period of time in the interests of efficiency. He may also order two or more co-operative societies to amalgamate or he may order large co-operatives to split up, all in the interests of the efficiency of the movement. The Commissioner is empowered to scrutinize, for approval or rejection, all budgets and proposals for major transactions by the co-operatives, in order to prevent any unwisely planned investments and/or undertakings by the co-operatives. Cheques drawn by the co-operatives are subject to scrutiny by the Commissioner or his field representative before being signed by these persons in order to make them valid.

The Role of Co-operatives in Kenya's Rural Areas

The Government accepts that the co-operative movement has a very important role to play in the development of the rural areas and in particular the small-scale farming areas. Needless to say, the movement is most active in these areas, where co-operatives are engaged in a wide range of activities involving the production, processing, handling and marketing of various farm and livestock products, in addition to offering some essential services, such as short-term production-credit facilities, tractor-hire services and the supply of inputs for production, such as fertilizers, seed and agricultural chemicals. In the interests of their farmer members, the co-operatives make advances for payments for essential social services, such as school fees, taxes and medical bills. It is quite obvious, therefore, that the role of the co-operatives is essential from the developmental and the socio-economic points of view in the rural areas.

The Department of Co-operative Development recognizes that the co-operative movement is, by and large, one of the most effective means of channelling credit to the small-scale farmers for rural development, and also it recognizes that, by encouraging thrift among the farmers and the salaried employees, in both the urban and the rural areas, through savings and credit societies, significant contributions towards the acceleration of rural development can be achieved. Currently the Co-operative Bank of Kenya is giving short-term credit to members through the movement under the popular

Co-operative Production Credit Scheme, a scheme which is under the scrupulous direction of the Department. There is already a great demand for the extension of the scheme, because it has proved successful and worth while. The estimated requirements for the scheme are expected to rise from approximately K£ 0.5 million for 1971 to K£ 1.75 million by 1974.

Apart from its credit activities, the Department of Co-operative Development is also engaged in activities to promote the development of a truly independent and self-reliant movement in Kenya. Educating members and the co-operative employees is, by and large, one of the Department's most vital undertakings, since it is believed that the long-term solution to the wide range of problems faced by the co-operatives lies in education for all.

Efficiency and Efficiency Problems in Co-operatives

Time and again, it has been stated that co-operatives have to be run as businesses, and indeed in no way contrary to sound business management. It is quite true that some of our co-operatives are rapidly growing and acquiring the size and stature of "truly big businesses" and are dealing in amounts running into millions of shillings. Consequently, they require management of the same high calibre as that of large private enterprises. It is obvious therefore that among the major factors for consideration, in discussing efficiency problems as they affect the co-operative movement, are management, education, leadership, loyalty and integrity.

1. *Management.* As well as being proficient business executives, co-operative managers need to be familiar with the products handled by their organisations; they should be aware of the problems facing their co-operators and they should keep abreast of matters relating to marketing and market situations in and outside their territorial boundaries. However, such high-calibre personnel for the managerial posts may definitely be expected to demand high remunerations. Private enterprises usually offer appropriate salaries, according to their

requirements, and so must the co-operatives, if they are to compete and to make their presence felt in the business world.

2. *"Felt economic need."* Many a time, collective statements are made by farmer groups when difficulties in the marketing of their products arise. One very common statement often heard is "... Let us form a co-operative to handle this and that etc.". Co-operatives formed in such haphazard ways usually do not go far, either in overcoming the immediate problems or in providing machinery for coping with the problems which they were formed to cope with. The need to investigate whether or not the "felt economic need" for forming such co-operatives ever existed should not be overlooked in discussing efficiency.

3. *Member support.* Loyal support, founded on intelligent decision-making procedures, is perhaps the single, most salient factor that determines the efficiency of a co-operative. If the co-operative does not offer any economic advantage to the members, the degree of co-operation will be low and since a co-operative usually depends upon the active participation of its members to use its services and/or for patronage, the members' interest must be aroused and maintained, if success is to be assured.

4. *Records.* Adequate record-keeping is a must. Like any other business, a co-operative should not be run with anything short of stringent record-keeping practices. Records are needed to provide members with information as to how their business is progressing. It is not uncommon to hear that certain co-operatives' books of accounts have not been audited for a period of many years, which definitely indicates that these co-operatives have kept no proper records for the purposes which are vital in all business undertakings. Efficiency cannot be expected to exist under such circumstances.

5. *Financing.* Financing should be arranged and planned to meet basic needs, which must first be defined clearly enough to be understood by the ordinary peasant farmer. The essential explanation should include the description of fixed assets desired, for example, land, buildings and equipment, and operating expenses, such as salaries and general operating costs, which are often not taken into account when new co-operatives are being planned by the public, an oversight which

may result in the misappropriation of funds set aside for the capital expenses. The recent involvement of farm-purchase co-operatives in Kenya in numerous financial entanglements and in fraudulent financial operations serves to exemplify the importance of the financing aspect.

6. *Volume of business.* A common weakness and a general drawback to the movement's progress is the lack of proper knowledge of the volume of business that any particular co-operative has or expects to have within a given period of time. The obvious need for appropriate volume assessment arises when one takes into consideration items for expenses that must be incurred whether the co-operative's activities are in or out of season. Fixed costs, such as the rent for buildings, the manager's salary, office expenses and the upkeep of factories and equipment, have to be met all the time. The volumes of effort and business are alike related to the costs and cannot be divorced in the assessment of efficiency.

The volume of business must provide for meeting the fixed costs and essential variable costs in all business undertakings. The volume of business beyond the aforementioned minimum usually goes to reduce the variable costs of production and for profit-making.

7. *Leadership.* The principles of democratic control which are expressed by the "one man, one vote" doctrine should be the foundation for the co-operative movement's administrative organisation. To ensure democractic control and to prevent what might be called "capitalistic control", co-operators participate and are involved in the broad decision-making processes that govern the running of the co-operative business in principle. However, the more important aspect of leadership appears to deviate from the democratic ideals and unfortunately excessive powers have been acquired by some leaders acting on their own or in collusion with others and have resulted in the misuse of the societies' properties in the name of "leadership". In accordance with the functions of the executive, a leader's duties include setting a good example to others in his organisation and being an individual whose moral standards are high and worthy of imitation by those whom he leads.

Co-operatives in Kenya have many times been subjected to violent criticism and have very rarely been praised, though sometimes quite exuberantly. The causes of condemnation and praise must be investigated, for no doubt there is something unique in the co-operative philosophy and its application in developing countries such as ours.

The problems facing co-operatives are of a complex and multi-dimensional nature. They must be given attention by governments from the village to the international level and a proper diagnosis must be made, in view of the desire that the co-operative movement should serve as a true vehicle for the development and uplifting of the under-privileged masses throughout the world.

The Kenyan Department of Co-operative Development has recently embarked upon field or applied research, because it is felt that the transfer of such research results directly to the field would produce the best effects, in view of the fact that the setting for the research is not only similar to that in which the results will be applied but is actually the same. We have therefore, as a matter of priority, organised research teams to carry out

(*a*) A district survey to map out the factors which affect co-operative development, adversely or otherwise, in each district.

(*b*) A merchandise survey to find out the influx and distribution of agricultural inputs which are vital to farming in the small-holder section.

(*c*) An economic survey to reveal the specific managerial/economic bottlenecks in particular co-operatives, with a view to rectifying situations before they deteriorate.

J. J. Musundi

Efficiency Problems in Kenyan Co-operatives

In submitting a paper on the subject of efficiency problems, it is worth while making an appraisal of the historical development of the co-operative movement in Kenya since the formation of co-operatives based on the money economy, as we know it to-day. Of course, this does not preclude the fact that the spirit and ideals of co-operation, based on African socialism, were inherent among the African population.

The first co-operative enterprises to be founded in Kenya started at the turn of this century, just before the outbreak of the first world war, through the spontaneous efforts of the former expatriate European settlers. The co-operatives which were established at that time were mainly for the purpose of marketing members' produce and supplying them with agricultural farm requisites.

The Kenya Farmers' Association (Co-operative) was one of the first co-operatives societies to be established. After the publication of the first Co-operative Societies Ordinance of 1931, the present countrywide co-operative organisations, like the Kenya Co-operative Creameries, the Kenya Farmers' Association and the Kenya Planters' Co-operative Union, were registered as co-operative societies.

However, the founders of these early co-operatives were discriminatory in nature, in that the statutes of their co-operatives were designed so as to exclude the participation of African peasant farmers. The situation was afterwards rectified

---

J. J. Musundi is the Secretary-General of the Kenya National Federation of Co-operatives, Nairobi.

through political changes in the country and now these organisations are controlled by the *Wananchi* (citizens) and not as described in Hyden and Karanja's book, *Rural Co-operatives and Planned Change in Africa* (page 168).

The composition of the membership of the three organisations has changed tremendously as a result of changes of ownership of land and the action taken by new African leaders in these bodies. Between 60% and 80% of the membership of each of these countrywide organisations is African. For instance, the management of the KPCU is almost all African.

Formation of Co-operatives in Rural Areas

It was not until the late 'forties that co-operative societies were established in the African rural areas, well known in the colonial era as "the African land units". The co-operative enterprises were initiated by the colonial government after an investigation which established the need for the formation of such institutions and the promulgation of the 1945 Co-operation Ordinance, which defined the lines on which the societies had to operate.

It should be remembered, however, that, prior to this period, which was beset with many economic and social problems after the second world war, the African peasant farmers were at the mercy of unscrupulous Asian traders, who exploited the farmers in the absence of an organised marketing system. The free marketing system provided conditions which were favourable for traders to pay peasant farmers very low prices for their agricultural produce. As far as the African farmers were concerned, efficiency was non-existent in their operations. Private traders normally purchased produce, such as maize, at prices between 1.50 shs. and 4.50 shs. per bag of 200 lb, which in turn realised prices of shs. 7.00 and shs. 9.00 per bag of the same weight. The Government was aware of this practice and decided to set up a statutory marketing board for handling maize and other produce under the name of the Maize Marketing Board and in the form of compulsory co-operation.

It was on account of this form of exploitation, coupled with the colonial-government policy in mobilising the economic efforts of peasant farmers for development purposes, that some initiative was taken to establish co-operative societies from the top downwards.

It can, however, be said that the break-through period of co-operatives in Kenya came after the Co-operative Societies Ordinance of 1945, which made it possible for co-operatives to spring up like mushrooms in the main producing areas of agricultural potential.

Having realised the importance of co-operative organisations in rural development among smallholder peasant farmers, the Government set up a Department of Co-operative Development, whose duties were to promote and supervise co-operative societies. However, the Department was handicapped by lack of staff and therefore its work made no significant impact on the population. This was due to the fact that Government officers were spared for other duties, such as the rehabilitation and training of ex-servicemen, and hence the work of promoting co-operatives in rural areas received little prominence in the initial stages. Secondly, the Department was regarded as a step-child which was of little importance in the government machinery (cf. Hyden 1970).

Introduction of Cash Crops

Some of the very early co-operatives which were attempted were the egg circles in the Nyanza Province of western Kenya (comprising the present Nyanza and Western Provinces). These societies encountered a lot of difficulties, as they were open to severe competition from the private traders. The egg circles eventually failed miserably, due to lack of managerial know-how and Government protection.

The Government later decided to intensify farming and accelerate agricultural production in the African rural areas. Farmers, producers' and marketing co-operatives were established to handle cash crops such as maize and coffee, particularly in the Central and Nyanza Provinces.

Notable among the early producers' and marketing societies were those which came under the Meru Coffee Co-operative

Union, the Kisii Farmers' Co-operative Union and the Embu Co-operative Union. Later co-operatives emerged under the Elgon Nyanza Farmers' Co-operative Union, the Kiambu Coffee Growers' Co-operative Union, the Nyeri Coffee-marketing Co-operative Union and the Murang'a Farmers' Co-operative Union, which were founded in the late 'fifties with a View to handling members' produce, such as coffee and maize.

Although the African peasant farmers were encouraged by the Government to form co-operative societies and this led to the establishment of several societies, their operation was difficult and trying, owing to the lack of experience and managerial knowhow, and consequently many of them fell by the wayside.

Management Problems

The efficiency problems which confronted these co-operative unions and societies were mainly managerial. For instance, in the late 'fifties, the Kisii Farmers' Co-operative Union, which was a very prosperous and well-managed organisation, faced some efficiency problems, which arose as a result of some misunderstanding between the committee and the manager. The committee later made the conditions unfavourable for the manager to continue in the service of the Union.

Another case in which efficiency problems were experienced was the Mt. Elgon Nyanza Farmers' Co-operative Union, once hailed by the Registrar of Co-operatives in the colonial period as one of the best-run co-operative unions in the country. It suffered a great setback after the committee decided to appoint one of their own number as the manager of the Union; to a certain degree this action demoralised the staff. The committee also tended to favour some individual members of staff. There was a lack of stock control for goods purchased for resale and the Union sustained heavy losses in this connection.

The problems of co-operative efficiency became more pronounced after Kenya had attained its political independence. Co-operatives became the source of the much-needed finance, which was expended on buying property, such as land and buildings, which were many miles away from the areas of operation, as stipulated in the bye-laws of the societies.

In most cases, the members' money from crop sales was directed to buying such property for speculative purposes. The principle of democratic control was seriously abused, in view of the fact that decisions to divert members' funds to other ventures were made by committee members without seeking the approval of the general membership.

The Department of Co-operative Development was very often called upon to register new societies purely on political criteria. The farm-purchase co-operative societies, which were founded during this period, were registered without sufficient economic investigation having been carried out to determine their future operations. Farm-purchase co-operative societies have been a constant source of political problems. The case of the Nyagocho Chisaro Chikunorwe Farmers' Co-operative Society, with nearly 12 000 members, is just one example which illustrates the problems of farm-purchase societies.

In consequence of these problems, it has been suggested that the farm-purchase co-operatives should be de-registered and turned into directed limited companies. I think that this would be a wrong approach to solving the problem. This is the best form of producers' society. All that is required is to regularise their operation, by reviewing their bye-laws to enable the active members, who are normally in the minority, to make some decisions in the absence of non-participating members.

Another aspect of the problems of efficiency is that which affects the accounts of co-operatives. For example, in Kenya, as late as 1969, several co-operatives had not had their books of account audited for several years. It was estimated that the co-operatives were nearly 2 500 years in arrears with audits of their accounts. This is an alarming figure indeed and it suggests that the co-operatives which were affected could not afford to declare bonuses for their members. This deficiency was necessitated by the fact that the Department of Co-operative Development was grossly understaffed and also could not attract qualified accountants, due to the low salary scales, particularly as professional accountants were scarce. Secondly, the professional private auditors who audited the societies' books were too slow and expensive.

Problems of Efficiency

Some efficiency problems are a result of poor planning in getting co-operatives established and registered without carrying out the proper groundwork. In Kenya, this is evidenced by the fact that hardly a week passes without the names of co-operative societies due for liquidation appearing in the *Official Gazette*.

Although the number of registered co-operative societies in Kenya stands at slightly above 1900, the number of active societies is only 800, which indicates that the majority of the co-operatives suffer from mismanagement.

There is, however, no doubt that the problems of efficiency can be surmounted by taking a more serious look at the operations of the existing societies, with a view to amalgamating the weak and unviable societies, either on a locational or a divisional basis and, in the case of co-operative unions, on the provincial level. Action taken in this regard would lead to the creation of co-operative societies and unions which are viable and functional. If the objective of creating viable units is to gain prestige, this would not be meaningful, but, if the purpose is to render efficient services and reduce costs to members, such action would be appreciated.

The concept of building multi-purpose co-operatives has been accepted in Kenya. The Nyeri District Co-operative Union was built on this pattern of a large unit which absorbed three different unions. Although the performance of the Nyeri Union has not come up to expectation, it is the best form of building co-operative to supplement the private business organisations. However, the building of too large organisations, in which there is no proper delegation of duties through departmental heads, could make the organisations unwieldy and less effective.

Government Control and Efficiency

It will be seen that the role which the Government plays in the promotion of co-operatives is an important one, without which the development of the co-operative movement in Kenya would have been completely retarded. As a result of the constant mismanagement of co-operatives, in which members' funds were spent without any regard being paid to the members, the Government took stern measures to curb these malpractices, which had become quite prevalent.

The Government brought in the Co-operative Societies Act of 1966, which gave the Commissioner for Co-operative Development more controlling powers. Co-operatives were required under the new Act to submit to the Commissioner annual budgets of revenue and expenditure and monthly trial balances. The Act also gave the Commissioner power to remove a society's committee, when he considered that it was not serving the interests of the members, and to replace the democratically elected committee with his own committee.

In exercising his powers under the Act, the Commissioner has removed the committees of a number of co-operatives, for instance, those of the Masaba Farmers' Co-operative Union, the Mt. Elgon Bungoma District Co-operative Union and the Nyagacho Chisaro Chikunorwe Farmers' Co-operative Society, in an endeavour to salvage the co-operatives concerned.

If the Government control is not enforced rigidly, there is less danger, but if it is applied without improving efficiency, it may create discontent and make the members apathetic and un-co-operative.

Effects of Government Control

I feel that, when it becomes necessary for the Government to take over the control of a co-operative organisation, it should ensure that such measures are applied only for a limited period of time and should then hand over the institution to the members in a viable form. When this is done, confidence will be restored. However, if the Government fails to improve the efficiency of the co-operative, members may lose confidence in it and this may lead to a complete failure of the whole organisation.

In this context, it may be worth while citing the case of the Mt. Elgon Bungoma District Co-operative Union, in which the members have not been satisfied with the take-over of the management of their Union, in view of the fact that the Government committee failed to bring about an improvement in the management of the Union during its first year under Government control.

When the Commissioner for Co-operative Development withdrew his control over the Masaba Farmers' Co-operative Union, the members of the Union were extremely pleased and, to indicate that they were not wholly in agreement with the Government take-over, they voted out all the members who had served on the Commissioner's committee, when elections were held for a new committee. There have been occasions when Government officers have misinterpreted the Act, by removing democratically elected committees of societies in favour of their own committees, as a result of which relations between the officers and the committee have been strained.

Another slightly different case in which efficiency problems were experienced was in the Meru Farmers' Co-operative Union, which was one of the largest co-operative unions in the country. They were due to some misunderstanding between the committee members and members in different areas, as a result of a demand for an additional seat on the committee for one area to be effectively represented. These differences eventually prompted the Minister for Co-operatives and Social Services to institute an inquiry into the affairs of the Union and on the recommendation of the commission of inquiry the Union was split into three unions.

Perhaps if the area which was inadequately represented on the management committee had been allowed an additional seat at the appropriate time, it would not have been necessary to consider splitting up the Union. In fact, that situation would have been averted if the Government had acted promptly, by advising the parties concerned. Although the splitting of the Union was justified, it made a mockery of the concept of multi-purpose unions.

However, Government control also helps to locate errors which might be made by co-operatives, as was the case in the Embu Co-operative Union a few years ago, when members were overpaid for their coffee crop by the Union and through

Government action a catastrophe was averted in the organisation.

Co-operatives have been said to be the best form of institution for promoting economic and social development, because of their application of the principle of democratic control, as opposed to the private institutions. Where co-operatives are efficient, they provide better solutions in most circumstances, particularly in the handling of members' produce, whereby costs are spread among many members and efficiency is secured by the centralisation of transportation services, accounting and supplies. The Kiambu Coffee Growers' Co-operative Union, and the Kirinyaga District Co-operative Union are typical examples in Kenya.

Competition with Private Traders and Members' Loyalty

However, co-operatives have not been a good solution in areas where there has been open competition with private traders, for instance, in the Coast and Western Provinces of Kenya, where co-operatives have failed to satisfy the members, because they did not pay them promptly and fairly.

Co-operatives have not been able to pay a higher price than private traders for crops like maize and other produce, where the Maize and Produce Board allows a traders' commission to its appointed agents. In general, co-operatives have retained most of the traders' commission, without passing some percentage of it on to members, because of high overhead costs.

In areas where it is not compulsory for members to sell their produce through co-operatives, members have never been loyal and, even where co-operatives were in competition with traders, members have tended to be disloyal to their societies, especially when incentives have not been given.

Efficiency through Education

Through education and training, co-operatives have achieved efficiency in their operations. Education provides better understanding between the members and the staff and this improves efficiency.

Co-operatives with trained staff, officials and members have operated more efficiently than those with less trained people. Where co-operatives have trained management staff with a view to improving their efficiency, they have succeeded better than those which have trained their personnel with a view to granting them extra benefits. In the majority of cases, when the expectations were not realized, co-operatives have been deserted by the trained personnel, who have sought for more lucrative posts in the private sector.

Election of Committee Members

The system of electing committee members in the co-operative organisations in Kenya varies very much. In some cases, where representation on the committee is based on areas, election to the committee is normally not influenced by factors such as clan etc. but purely on the merits of individuals.

In some of the national co-operatives, an alternative means which may be employed in electing committee members is through the representation of delegates at the annual general meeting, while maintaining the principle of "one man, one vote".

At times, pressures have been mounted and co-operatives with large memberships or share-holdings, particularly in the national organisations, have demanded to be given more voting powers at general meetings.

1. *Research Priorities*

Co-operatives were established in East Africa under the British colonial rule at varying periods. It can be said that no thorough survey was carried out to determine the extent to which traditional co-operative ideals were related to the economic and social concept. In some cases, co-operatives were established without any serious attempt being made to motivate the would-be members to take the initiative in forming such institutions. For many years, scholars in East Africa were concerned about other aspects of development than the contribution which co-operatives were making to the economic and social development of the countries of the region. The co-operative enterprises which had any chance of success in all the three East African countries were the farmers', producers' and marketing organisations. Despite the fact that these co-operatives met with some competition from the private traders, they made a very big impact on the farming community, in view of the services which they rendered to members.

2. *Co-operative versus State-owned Corporations*

It is stated in the Co-operative Societies Act of Kenya that, where co-operatives handle more than 60% of an agricultural product, such an area most be declared a co-operative area. While the Government has agreed to promote co-operatives and to use them as the best vehicles for mobilising the local resources for economic and social advancement, co-operatives are not given a free hand in their participation. Research should be carried out to determine whether co-operatives should be the only institutions to handle agricultural produce from producers until it reaches the consumers, without passing through state-controlled corporations, or whether they should content themselves with operating on an agency basis.

Where co-operatives have proved to be efficient in processing and marketing an agricultural commodity, there should be less Governmental participation in marketing such a commodity. For instance, in Kenya, coffee co-operatives handle the crop right from production to the point of sale, when it is handed over to the Coffee Board of Kenya, which sells the crop at open auction through the brokers. Research workers should be able to show whether there is any justification for the existence of statutory bodies, when the crops could well be handled by the co-operative movement and thereby the duplication of functions and increased overhead costs to the producers could be avoided.

3. *Information about Co-operatives*

Co-operatives have been in existence in Kenya for nearly 26 years, as far as the rural areas are concerned, and some of them have proved to be successful in their activities, yet the ignorance that exists among both members and non-members is colossal. Research should be undertaken, to look into the question of whether the methods used in informing members and the public are effective enough and also whether the co-operative members receive sufficient incentives to induce them to patronise their associations.

4. *Management Efficiency*

It has been said too often that the success of co-operative enterprise depends on the managerial skills which are employed in running the co-operatives. In Kenya, very few co-operative unions can afford to attract highly qualified people as managers.

Because the co-operatives are the people's institutions, very often members do not approve of money being spent on staff-training. In some cases, it is considered a waste of money. It should be possible for research to reveal the amount and level of training that should be given to the management staff of the co-operative movement.

If co-operatives have to be run on business lines, like private organisations, high-level management training should be provided for the staff.

It has been claimed that, in some co-operatives in Kenya, management efficiency has been affected by the fact that co-operative employees and managerial staff tend to improve their own economic positions at the expense of members. This has been experienced in co-operatives which handle such crops as coffee and maize. Through research, it may be possible to find out the reasons which prompt managements and committees to prefer to serve their own personal interests.

For instance, there have been allegations that managerial and clerical staff in societies which handle coffee have taken advantage of those members who are illiterate, by cheating them in giving them low weights for their produce, in order to improve their own financial positions. This may not be a serious problem, but it may have a tremendous effect on the members.

5. *Organisational Structure of Co-operatives*

The main emphasis in the development of the co-operative movement in East Africa has mainly been on producers' marketing co-operatives. Indeed, these organisations have been successful, by and large, at all the different levels, namely, at the primary and secondary levels. This development has been desirable, but with the increasing immigration of the rural population into the urban areas there is undoubtedly a need to carry out a survey of consumers' co-operation in both urban and rural areas.

Through research, it will be possible to incorporate consumers' co-operation, with a view to avoiding a state of affairs in which there is duplication of resources, either intellectual or financial. Of course, the purpose of such research would be to determine the problem areas and to suggest the solutions and goals to be attained.

6. *Industrialisation of Rural Co-operation*

Whilst great importance has been attached to the marketing co-operative societies, which handle agricultural produce in East Africa, little has been said about producers' or industrial co-operatives, particularly in the rural areas.

The population increase at the rate of 3% annually in Kenya, coupled with the high rate of unemployment, poses a major problem to the country. Although efforts are being made to reduce the birth rate by scientific methods of family-planning, these methods do not provide immediate solutions to this problem.

As more young men and women leave the schools after their secondary education and come into the world, the burden of finding jobs for them becomes increasingly onerous. It is in this context that co-operatives should venture to provide some occupational activities for the new generation.

Research should be undertaken to look into the possibilities of initiating primary industries for processing some of the agricultural products. Of course, to be able to embark on such undertakings, it will be necessary to create the infrastructure to make such industries possible.

Because of their unique position, co-operatives could provide an atmosphere of entrepreneurship, by pioneering the industrialisation of rural areas and thereby creating employment to meet the growing need. This could be done by the joint participation of the co-operatives and the Government. This may sound utopian, but it is appropriate that co-operatives in this region should be concerned about the processing of agricultural products for industrial purposes and should engage in producers' (industrial) co-operatives in handicrafts, pottery, etc.

It will be necessary to carry out feasibility studies of cottage or small-scale industries simultaneously with the market research for the finished products. This may seem like a departure from the planned rural economy based on the agricultural industry. However, it will have a supplementary effect on the rural co-operative efforts already in existence and on those planned for future development. These are but a few of the areas where research should be given priority.

A Short History of the Co-operative Movement in Mauritius

During the first decade of this century, small-scale sugar-cane planters were experiencing considerable hardships in securing cultivation loans. They had to pay exorbitant rates of interest, ranging from 60% to 120% per annum, with a mortgage on their lands and their dreaded conditional sale, in default of repayment, thrown in. Advantage was also taken of their illiteracy, their indifference to keeping accounts and their ignorance of business practices. The Royal Commission of 1909 recommended the setting up of co-operative banks to come to their rescue. As a result, an expert, Mr S. Wilberforce, of the Indian Civil Service, recommended special legislation for their constitution and control and thus Ordinance No. 4 of 1913 was enacted.

These societies, based on the Raiffaisen model, with unlimited liabilities, in which each member is responsible for the debts of every other member, were only concerned with providing agricultural loans to small cane planters under the control of the Director of Agriculture. Moreover, as these co-operatives were sponsored by the Government, and taking also into account the distressing conditions of the planters whom they were expected to assist, it was natural that they had to be financed by the Government.

In the initial stages, progress was extremely slow and, in 1915, only 20 societies were in existence. Ten years later, in 1923, the number of societies had increased to 36, but loans outstanding had risen from Rs 1 164 in 1915 to Rs 62 834. The movement then took a downward plunge and by 1932 the number of societies had decreased to 28, but loans overdue had climbed to Rs 160 561. Corrective measures had to be taken to prevent the movement from being a complete failure.

The Co-operative Division of the Department of Agriculture was re-organised; additional staff were enlisted, a full-time Assistant Registrar was appointed, greater supervision and control were exercised, and the Ordinance was amended in 1935. The situation was further improved by the promulgation of the Cane Sale & Purchase Ordinance in 1939, which resulted ultimately in the linking of credit with the marketing of canes. The change was dramatic. In 1944 the number of societies rose to 66 and the percentage of default had been reduced from 60% in 1932 to 2.1%. The Agricultural Credit Movement has now become the backbone of co-operation in Mauritius. At the close of the financial year ended 28 February 1969, the 175 societies on the register, including 19 in Rodrigues, had a membership of 13 252, as against 1 486 in 1914. Share capital rose from Rs 52 721 in 1914 to Rs 553 589, while reserves stood at Rs 2 699 301 in comparison with Rs 2 312 in 1914. Crop loans issued during the year amounted to Rs 6 266 230, as against Rs 115 504 in 1914.

The year 1945 marked a turning-point in the local history of co-operatives. It received a visit from Mr W.K.H. Campbell, former Registrar of Co-operative Societies, Ceylon, who came to enquire into the co-operative movement and to advise the Government on the steps to be taken for its improvement. The new legislation which was passed on his recommendation (Ordinance No. 51 of 1945) widened the scope of co-operative activities and made provision for the registration of all types of co-operative societies. In view of these developments, a separate Department of Co-operation was created in 1947 under a full-time Registrar, vested with the following responsibilities: (i) registration, arbitration and liquidation, (ii) inspection and certification, and (iii) promotion and education.

Co-operative stores made their appearance in 1947. Built up at a time when rationing due to the war was still prevalent, the consumer movement made rapid strides, because, in a large measure, of the rapacity of its competitors. In 1949 the Mauritius Co-operative Wholesale Society Ltd was registered to cater for the needs of the co-operative stores and to reap the additional benefits of wholesaling. By 1962 the consumer movement reached its highest mark: 79 societies were in operation, comprising 14 598 members and with a turnover of Rs 6 757 061.

The Wholesale Society had a turnover of Rs 4 580 533. But the movement was not to escape its share of troubles. The greatest obstacles have been lack of efficient management and abuse of credit sales. By 1963, the credit extended to members had absorbed most of the working capital of a substantial number of co-operative stores, a fact which meant that they were heavily indebted to the M.C.W.S. What with the lack of working capital and the widespread distress as a result of repeated cyclones, 20 stores had to be de-registered in 1965. The M.C.W.S. itself became another victim and, in spite of the remedial measures taken to save it, it had to go into liquidation in November 1967. The situation has since then been slowly improving, thanks to the efficiency of a dozen stores. On 28 February 1969, turnover from the 57 stores in operation, including two in Rodrigues, amounted to Rs 7 460 698, an excess of three-quarters of a million rupees over the figure for the previous peak year (1962).

In 1948, a most notable event took place—the creation of the Mauritius Co-operative Central Bank Ltd, which has become the mainstay of the co-operative movement. It was felt that, for the movement to develop along sound lines, it was not possible to continue relying upon Government funds and that the movement had to set up its own financing agency. Registered with a capital of Rs 19 792, the M.C.C.B. has not ceased to make steady progress. In its first year of operation, it advanced loans to its members to the value of Rs 779 094, thanks to a floating overdraft of Rs 1 000 000 from Barclays Bank. In 1969, loans disbursed amounted to Rs 5 704 439 and the share capital and reserves have gone up to Rs 2 391 275. In addition, the Bank has managed to attract deposits from members and non-members to the tune of Rs 5 005 708.

Restricted to short-term crop loans at the beginning, the Bank has kept on improving its services to its patrons. Medium-term loans were introduced in 1963 to redeem onerous mortgages and to provide assistance in purchasing new lands; bull-dozing loans were introduced in 1968 to increase productivity; long-term loans were also made available to finance co-operative housing societies in 1963. Furthermore, the Bank has recently been affiliated to the International Co-operative Banking Co. Ltd (INGEBA) at Basle, Switzerland. The objects of all these efforts are to serve its members in a more efficient and adequate manner.

Another secondary society to be set up was the Mauritius Co-operative Agricultural Federation Ltd, established in 1950 to promote the agricultural interests of planters. It had obtained representation on the various statutory boards set up to regulate the sugar, tobacco and tea industries.

The Mauritius Co-operative Union Ltd, which is the top national body of the movement, was registered in 1952. Its main function is to provide education and training. It also undertakes publicity and propaganda and operates a small cinema unit. It has also made staff available to the Department of Co-operation to assist in the supervision of accounts. From 1962 to 1965, regular courses were run at the Union on such subjects as book-keeping, co-operative law, basic economics, the principles and ideals of co-operation and other allied subjects. Unfortunately, these courses were discontinued for lack of funds.

Other forms of co-operative endeavour have also come into existence since the green light was given by the enactment of the 1945 Ordinance. Co-operative thrift and savings societies were formed in 1948 to encourage people to save. The 11 societies in operation have 1 429 members, with deposits totalling Rs 270 770. Co-operative school savings banks were started in 1952 to encourage the habit of thrift in young people. There are at present in Mauritius 12 such societies, with 2 716 pupils and deposits of Rs 13 258. However, in Rodrigues seven such schools with 1 819 pupils have deposits amounting to Rs 18 587. The latest development in the field of savings is the formation of credit unions, of which 11 are now in full operation. The object is to save wage-earners from the clutches of unscrupulous money-lenders.

Co-operative housing societies enable members to possess their own houses by advancing them long-term loans at reasonable rates of interest. The three societies on the register have been responsible for the construction of 129 houses. There is no doubt that only the shortage of long-term capital is preventing them from expanding.

Co-operative transport societies were set up in 1952 to transport members' canes during the crop season. The 11 societies, with 672 members, had a turnover of Rs 183 524 in 1969. Also worth mentioning is the Co-operative Printing Society, with a turnover of Rs 70 120 in 1969.

Two types of co-operative societies have not been particularly successful—those for fishermen and shoemakers. Lack of capital and absence of proper education and marketing facilities have been the main obstacles.

The latest types of co-operatives are the marketing societies for tea, the marketing societies for potatoes and onions and the pig-marketing societies.

The La Chartreuse Tea Marketing Co-operative Society consists of 14 members with 1 424 arpents under tea cultivation and also operates the former Government tea factory, which it took over in 1967. In 1969, it exported tea to the value of Rs 2 255 379 and marketed tea locally for Rs 145 624. Smallholders in the Government Tea Development Project are grouped in five tea credit and marketing societies, consisting of 371 members holding 1 291 arpents. Societies of this type may become the model for future development, catering for the unemployed settled on Government lands.

The co-operative marketing societies for potatoes and onions were formed after the setting up of the Agricultural Marketing Board, in order to enable small producers to enjoy the benefits of group action in the marketing of their produce. When the Marketing Board operated single-channel marketing, they were the agents of the Board and their members had to contract with them for the disposal of their produce. Such an arrangement facilitated the provision of production credit from the Mauritius Co-operative Central Bank Ltd. When the Board withdrew from commercial operations, the Government had to guarantee their loans from the M.C.C.B. Their big problems at present are trying to organise proper marketing channels for the sales of their produce and trying to find capital to make advances to their members, whilst waiting for their produce to be sold. Such problems do not exist for the

Rodrigues Agricultural Production and Marketing Co-operative Society, as their onions, garlic and limes are purchased outright by the Agricultural Marketing Board at prices fixed in advance.

Small pig breeders in Mauritius experience many difficulties in obtaining credit and supplies; they are particularly vulnerable in the marketing of their produce, which they are compelled to dispose of at ridiculously low prices. These farmers have now turned to co-operatives for redress. In September 1970 was registered the Roche Bois Pig Credit and Marketing Co-operative Society. Since then eight more such societies have been organised and now in September 1971 they have formed themselves into a Federation, which, it is expected, will be in a better position to undertake the bulk marketing of their members' produce and thus to defend their interests more vigorously.

An attempt is also now being made to organise craftsmen, such as cabinet-makers, in co-operatives. It is too early to say whether such co-operatives will succeed here, the more so as there is no former experience in this field to draw upon.

Generally speaking, it can be said that the co-operative movement is very much alive in Mauritius. A boost was given to it last year by the setting up of a separate Ministry, known as the Ministry of Co-operatives and Co-operative Development. An educational programme was started in January 1971, in collaboration with the University of Mauritius, to train committee-men, staff and the general membership. Already there has been an awakening in the membership and a quickening of interest in the public. No doubt the movement is facing many problems, to a great many of which no ready solutions are available. Yet, on the whole, the future appears to be promising.

11 – 724148 *Widstrand*

P. Mauremootoo

The Position in Mauritius

One of the first impressions which strikes any outsider studying the Mauritius co-operative movement is the question of its ageing leadership. There can be no doubt that many of the leaders concerned have done yeoman service in the past to the cause of co-operation. They have displayed, in ample measure, an admirable crusading spirit. They have given many proofs of their goodwill and their sense of sacrifice. There is no denying the fact that their contribution to the present state of the co-operatives has been invaluable. Yet, after recognising all this, it must be agreed that they have also developed an attitude that they know best and now feel that without their continued presence in all key positions, the movement is bound to deteriorate. There is also, perhaps unconsciously, a feeling that their occupation of such positions is a justifiable reward for their past achievements and thus they find it hard to tolerate any challenge to their actual leadership.

1. The Leadership Crisis

This situation is bound to lead to certain conflicts. Times have changed. New problems are cropping up; problems derived from growth—that very growth which is to the credit of the old leaders. The question can then be posed: Is the bulk of the present leadership qualified to meet the new challenge? Inevitably, as co-operatives become a force to be

P. Mauremootoo is the Secretary of the Mauritius Co-operative Union Limited.

antagonising the old leaders. It is not yet clear whether a reckoned with, they are bound to run the gauntlet of their private competitors, who are already entrenched and in com- new type of leadership, informed, competent, adventurous. Only young leaders can provide such a leadership. The movement cannot afford the luxury of discarding the drive and enthusiasm of the young leaders.

The big concern for the movement is to provide opportunities to enable new leaders, in spite of their brashness and impatience, to serve the movement, without, at the same time, antagonising the old leaders. It is not yet clear whether a harmonious combination of the two groups can be worked out satisfactorily. What must be avoided at all costs is a state of affairs in which the movement is left without heirs.

There is another complication that results from the present state of affairs. In order to prepare young leaders to assume their responsibilities, there is a need to develop an educational programme. Though an attempt is being made in this direction, such a programme is not yet viewed with much sympathy by some leaders. There is a fear that they may be displaced by the new leaders coming up. Nor is that fear totally unjustified. There have been cases in which, after training, young managers and secretaries have offered their services to societies at cut rates. Consequently, it is no wonder that the educational programme is not getting all the support it deserves from certain influential leaders.

2. Management Problems

A major difficulty facing Mauritian co-operatives is in the field of management. The diversification of the movement from agricultural credit is comparatively recent. Co-operatives of the consumer and marketing types (fish, potatoes, onions, pigs) require knowledge and skill in their technical operations, in order to increase their efficiency, thereby maximising the benefits to their members. This country has up to now been unable to provide such technical know-how. The introduction of co-operative farming and industrial co-operatives (cabinet-making, leather work, metal work, etc.) is also being contemplated. The trouble is that there is no local experience in these fields on which to draw. There is a real possibility that the high hopes and enthusiasm of their prospective members may eventually founder on the rocks of inefficient and wasteful practices, in the absence of practical guidance on the "mechanics" of the business concerned. There is a case here for specialisation and for the provision of specialised training in particular business operations.

3. Research Requirements

In the field of research, nothing has been attempted. There is a need for studies to determine standards of performance. There is need for studies to ascertain the minimum costs of the many operations to be carried out in the business. At present, there is wide disparity in the cost effectiveness, depending on the quality of management.

The desirability of entering new sectors requires investigations, leading, where applicable, to the prior training of the necessary cadres. Certainly, feasibility studies should be carried out objectively and, where any project is not viable, it should not be attempted. There is a tendency at present to organise co-operatives in a haphazard manner, simply at the request of prospective members, on the ground that this is development. Invariably, in many instances, the guiding principle is based on goodwill and muddling through instead of knowledge and competence.

As for education and training also, there is need to research both the contents and the methods and to survey the audio-visual aids available elsewhere. Implementation can then depend on what is best, after due adaptation to local conditions and requirements. A corollary to the above is the education of trainers with the widest possible experience, in order to cope with a wide variety of situations.

4. General

There is no doubt that the co-operatives in Mauritius possess solid foundations and the necessary infrastructure, subject to improvements, for further development. However, such development must be on sound lines and must form part of a plan, wherein priorities are established and allocations of scarce resources are decided in advance. Unfortunately, such a development plan has not yet been formulated in Mauritius. The immediate requirements are the upgrading of the performance of existing co-operatives. Entry into new fields should be preceded by careful studies and analysis based on hard facts, the assembly of the expertise required and continuous support, at least in the early stages. Only in these circumstances, it is felt, can development proceed on smooth lines, avoiding bottlenecks and waste of effort and resources, and achieving efficiency in operation.

H. Ramdin

Efficiency Problems in Mauritius

At the very outset, it should be said that co-operatives started on the wrong foot under the colonial regime which obtained in Mauritius up to 1968. People with certain needs were grouped together and no attempt was made to get one or more suitable persons trained to run the show. Directions come from the top, i.e. the Government officers in charge of fostering the movement, with the inevitable bureaucracy which goes with the system. It is only recently that training courses have been started to get people trained for running co-operatives.

1. The Management Problems

Yet, even now, these courses are mainly concerned with in-service personnel. A very limited number of private candidates are admitted to these courses, which are run by the University of Mauritius jointly with the Mauritius Co-operative Union Limited. This set-up requires some re-formulation, in view of the diversification of the business of co-operatives in many directions and the need for imparting management skills of higher order to people who will be in charge of complex institutions like co-operative banks, supermarkets, etc. Whilst managers are now being trained, a different type of problem is emerging, in the fact that in a large number of cases trained persons are not being utilized on the jobs for which they have been trained. This is so because, in the race against time and the rush to make up for lost time, training is being given for

---

H. Ramdin is the Acting Registrar of Co-operative Societies in Mauritius.

the sake of training and not with any particular job in view. This is creating frustration among trained people and will have to be remedied.

2. Member Participation

It is a pity that in many cases the people have come to think that the object of the co-operative movement is to start co-operative societies and then to allow some dedicated people to conduct the business for them. Only the business side of these institutions is looked after.

The question of having co-operatives for self-help through mutual assistance and enthusiastic participation is secondary. This is why, so far, we have seen co-operatives set up to run a certain business as well as possible, without any extension into the various aspects of human relationships in the socio-economic fields, about which co-operatives should also concern themselves. People are apt to forget that co-operatives are measures designed to emancipate the weaker sections of the community, not only economically but also socially. We find that the people who form the greater part of the co-operatives lack the synthesis of the means and the ends needed to make the movement a really mass movement. This situation, it is hoped, will be remedied by mass education, using the mass media.

3. Technical-efficiency Problem

Co-operatives face the problem of personnel management, which itself is related to leadership and management development. Up to now, we have been faced with "one-man shows" in most co-operatives, with the result that they develop at the pace that the "one man" allows it. This is a very difficult field to tackle, especially as it involves men. There is the paradox that, as business institutions, co-operatives should keep employment costs to a minimum, whilst at the same time obtaining adequate and competent manpower to operate efficiently and expeditiously. Very few co-operatives ask themselves how many people they should employ, whom they should employ and how to get the best out of those who are employed. In other words, actual scientific management is lacking, to get the right personnel to achieve the objectives in view. There is no job analysis, no job evaluation and worse, in many cases, no proper selection and training. Employees of most of the credit societies are part-time people, who get a meagre stipend for their services and who do not look upon service in co-operatives as a career but as a stopgap in their searches for sources to supplement their main incomes. All the tools and techniques which have been evolved by scientific management and which are used by the private and public sectors to secure efficient management of their enterprises are not being used by our enterprises. This is the main technical-efficiency problem in Mauritius—that we have had, up to now, to accept mainly amateurs to run the co-operative enterprises. No doubt this has retarded progress, especially in the creation of large-sized and competitive co-operative organisations.

There is also the question of the uneven development of villages linked with this efficiency problem. This is the tragedy of it all, which must be remedied with proper education and training at all levels. Enlightening the masses about co-operative action is bound to accelerate the growth of efficient institutions, in which ideas (which have hands and feet, as we say at Coady) are bound to come up for further development on sound co-operative lines.

4. Research

No systematic research and study have been undertaken in co-operative training techniques. This factor is responsible for the delay in making the programmes more dynamic and suited to the needs of the present times and in making them effective instruments in future planning and development.

On the other side, with the growth of the movement, various practices and methods in the organisation and running of co-operatives have developed which need systematic studies and especially *experimentation,* with regard to their suitability for application in Mauritius. This task requires research workers and there is no doubt that the University of Mauritius can provide a suitable forum for research into co-operative problems and the techniques, forms and types best suited for our local conditions. It is about time that the University was encouraged to take up research or field studies on co-operatives.

Current Problems of Efficiency in the Performance of Co-operatives in Tanzania

A Joint Presentation by the Tanzanian Participants

We comment upon the problems in the light of the existing structure of the co-operative movement in Tanzania, which is basically an agricultural marketing movement, and also in the view of its future transformation into a production-based, multi-purpose movement, It should also be understood that in Tanzania, co-operatives are an integral part of national development, as highlighted by the national development of the party and the government.

In discussing efficiency in the performance of co-operatives, our attention is focussed on the optimum compromise between the role of expertise, on the one hand, and members' democratic participation, on the other.

In presenting these problems, it is assumed that the readers have already some idea of the achievements of the movement so far and its direction, as summarised in the interview with the Secretary-General of the Co-operative Union of Tanganyika (pp. 179–97). Reference should be made to the chapter dealing with the development of the co-operative movement in Tanzania in the *Handbook on Co-operative Education* (pp. 7–11).

Constitutional Problems

These are problems arising from the constitutional or legal framework regulating the work of co-operatives—mainly the primary societies—as contained in the Co-operative Societies Act and Societies Byelaws.

(*a*) Lack of a clear division of labour between the role of the members' elected representatives—the committee—at the primary level and that of the employed staff. Ideally, the role of the committee is, firstly, to make minor policy decisions and to give the management staff guidance and direction in carrying out their role in fulfilling the objectives of the society, as expressed in the byelaws and decisions of the general meetings; secondly, to delegate power and responsibility to the staff to execute the technical duties; and, thirdly, to provide motivation and co-ordination and to supervise and control the work of the staff.

The lack of clarity has resulted in the committee-men being involved in the daily routines of execution, for example, in produce- and cash-handling, so much so that the committee's ability to exercise effective control and to really become the members' watchdogs is greatly reduced and indeed substantially limited. In recent years, an attempt has been made in the field of consumer societies to distinctly separate the duties of the committee and those of the management. Experience from some selected societies shows promising results.

(b) Conflict between the powers of the members and those of the Registrar. Although members are supposed to have the final say on the affairs of their societies (through decisions made at general meetings), according to the Societies Act, the implementation of such members' decisions is subject to the Registrar's approval. There is thus a dilemma. While the purpose of involving the Registrar is to safeguard the interests of the members (taking into consideration their level of education), on the other hand, it tends to make the members feel that they have not much say in the control and direction of their societies. This results in indifference amongst members with regard to their positive responsibility for exercising the democratic control of their society. The impact of members' control, in the form of pressure-group action, over the performance of the committee and the management is weakened.

As a result of (*a*) and (*b*) above, the group feels there is a need to produce a Co-operative Law Manual, giving guidance on the interpretation of the Co-operative Societies Acts or Ordinances, for the purpose of solving the problems of efficiency which emerge as a result of ambiguous legislation.

Organisational and Operational Problems

As a result of ambiguous legal interpretation with respect to power relationships, difficulties also emerge in the distribution of powers in relation to responsibilities between committees and the staff. Thus, in the actual carrying out of various operations, it is difficult to identify which group should be held responsible for the results. Consequently, secretaries of primary societies (marketing) do not act as managers with powers to

(i) make managerial decisions,

(ii) assign duties to their fellow staff (assistant secretaries and other clerical assistants),

(iii) give instructions,

(iv) co-ordinate efforts, and

(v) organise effective communication.

Lacking power in organisational work, the staff assume it is the responsibility of the committee. But the committee, on the other hand, lack adequate management knowledge and business acumen. This is therefore a serious management deficiency of great concern.

Financial Problems

These arise from (i) the problem of optimum size in relation to manageable area of operation and (ii) the individual members' limited contribution to the capital resources of the society.

As regards the manageable size with respect to membership (social factor), a good number of societies have a relatively insufficient volume of business to generate adequate income to (i) attract the services of more highly skilled (qualified) staff and (ii) generate surpluses which could contribute to the building up of their reserves. These societies operate with insufficient financial resources.

Another factor which weakens the financial strength of many primary societies is the limitation of each individual member's contribution to the capital resources of their societies. Due to this inability to secure capital funds, some societies find it difficult to acquire such basic assets as godowns, which are essential in the maintenance of good-quality produce, the stoppage of shrinkage and the prevention of theft.

It should be observed that loss of produce quality or loss of produce by way of shrinkage or theft affects the final return to the farmers, which is one of the measurements of efficiency. Also the insufficient volume of turnover may also lead to increasing levies, in an attempt to cover operational costs, and consequently to a reduction of the farmers' cash return.

It should also be observed that lack of sufficient capital resources limits the abilities of the societies to offer more services to the members. The provision of more services would induce members to use their societies more frequently to satisfy their various needs and therefore would create a more favourable relationship and increase members' loyalty to their societies.

Attempts to counteract the limitation of size and members capital contributions have been made through the policy of amalgamation. These measures, however, create new management problems. Measures have also been taken to provide for additional capital resources through loans.

At this juncture it is important to take into account the possibilities that *Ujamaa* villages or production-based and multi-purpose societies offer with regard to the

(i) reduction of operational costs,

(ii) increased agricultural output through large-scale production, taking advantage of the economies of scale,

(iii) minimisation of financial losses on produce,

(iv) improved conditions for democratic participation and control by members,

(v) increased returns to farmers, and

(vi) better possibilities of generating and organising surpluses for development purposes.

Personnel Problems

(*a*) *Recruitment by the committees of primary societies.* According to the byelaws, it is the committee that has the power to employ staff. However, in most cases, committee-men lack both adequate basic education, literacy and business-management acumen. As a result, the decisions to employ staff are mainly based on personal relationships rather than scientific selection—hence the employment of unqualified staff or potentially capable staff.

(b) *Old employees.* These employees are still found in abundance in primary societies. The problem associated with this group is due to their limited capacity to adapt themselves to change. Because of their long on-the-job experience, they feel that they have nothing to learn and they do not readily respond to the needs for the further training necessary for fostering new managerial skills. On the other hand, as the old secretaries cannot be easily removed to make room for better-educated young ones or better-trained staff, this fact also contributes to reduce the possibilities of providing the necessary incentives and motivations needed to foster efficiency.

To counteract some of the problems mentioned above, it has been decided that all clerical staff who have not attended courses organised by the Co-operative College will have to study prescribed correspondence courses, followed by prescribed field courses, for the purpose of facilitating staff selection and training for primary societies. An attempt has been made to extend the idea of unified co-operative service to the societies affiliated to a co-operative union. To supplement this effort, consideration is being given to the idea of getting the co-operative unions to advise the primary societies in the recruitment of staff.

Accounting, Inspection and Audit Problems

Accounting, inspection and audit records are reckoned to be important means of providing essential information to facilitate effective management and members' democratic control. Thus, factors that restrict the availability of such records would therefore constitute problems of efficiency in the work of the co-operatives.

(a) Although in a good number of primary societies books of accounts are kept up to date, there are also a fair number of societies in which accounts are not kept up to date. This, in turn, will make it impossible to conduct a regular inspection of the affairs of these societies.

(*b*) Lack of uniform inspection reports providing relevant information which would facilitate prompt management action, where needed, is another factor affecting efficiency. This means that, even if books are kept up to date and regular inspections are carried out, the records will still not automatically reveal important information with regard to (i) the financial and (ii) the economic position of the society which is required by those involved in the supervisory and advisory functions, for example, the committees, the Co-operative Department staff and the union management.

In order to improve this situation, new inspection forms have been designed and it is hoped that they will help to solve the aforesaid problem in the future.

(*c*) The inadequacy of the inspectorate for carrying out regular inspections is a third factor. This means that, even if books are kept up to date and the appropriate inspection reports and programmes are available, the inadequacy will still constitute an inspection problem, in that not all societies will be inspected regularly for the purposes of detecting and rectifying deficiencies by those concerned.

(*d*) *Audit delays.* On account of the above-mentioned problems in accounting and inspection, final audited accounts cannot be produced in reasonably good time. This results in delays in presenting the final accounts and balance sheets and the subsequent distribution of the final proceeds to the members, and also in the lack of background information for assessing the past performance and for the planning of future activities. Furthermore, in the absence of audited accounts, it becomes difficult for societies to prove their economic and financial position for the purpose of obtaining development finance from the banks.

(*e*) *Method of presentation.* It is provided in the Act that it is the duty of the Registrar to audit or to cause to be audited the accounts of societies. For this reason, final audited accounts and statements are produced in a professional style, but when they are presented to the members for adoption, they have to be interpreted verbally to them at general meetings.

The outcome of this procedure is that members do not understand them sufficiently well to be able to use the information, on the basis of which they are supposed to exercise effective control.

It was therefore felt that the Registrar should require the auditors to produce two sets of final audited accounts, (*a*) a professional set and (*b*) a simplified version for information to members.

Research and Statistics

(*a*) Due to obvious delays in auditing accounts and because the Research Section at present depends wholly on the final accounts as the basis of its materials, there is the difficulty of preparing or compiling an up-to-date set of statistics.

(*b*) This leads to an overall lack of clarity as to the economic affairs of unions and societies, making it difficult to decide upon research priorities.

(*c*) Inability to use such data to activate the primary societies' members by presenting the data in a comparative way, i.e. comparing the performance of Society A with that of Society B.

(*d*) Further, there is the absence of a standardised system of accounting, which renders the comparison between societies and unions difficult.

Problems of Education and Training

Co-operative education and training comprise education and training for staff and committee-men, on the one hand, and information and enlightenment for members, on the other. The purpose of such educational activity is to foster skills and to instil knowledge for the efficient and effective running of the society's affairs. In order that co-operative education and training may contribute meaningfully to efficient performance, it should be undertaken by one co-ordinated approach.

Since co-operative societies are basically organisations of members, it may be assumed that priority should be given to education at the base. However, effective member education is best given by the tangible results which members achieve as a result of their co-operative action. This means that there must be an efficient leadership and management, if such tangible results are to be achieved. Consequently, it becomes imperative to organise committee and staff education, besides formal member education.

For the purposes of efficiency, money for education has to be spent on the right staff and committee, from whom the member may receive service benefits in proportion to his investment.

If such results are to be achieved, it is absolutely essential to apply methods of staff selection, training and promotion whereby staff are carefully selected and trained and then given the right incentives, by promotion, in terms of increased responsibilities, further education and attractive renumeration. This should apply to both the governmental staff involved in co-operative promotion and the staff of the co-operative societies. However, so far, this has not been the operative system in staff-training and education. A fair number of staff who have been trained but who have not been properly utilised have moved out of the movement or the government department to seek better prospects elsewhere or, if they have failed to find an alternative outlet, they have continued to work but with indifference, which means that the co-operative movement suffers a very substantial loss in terms of productivity.

In Tanzania, of course, attempts are being made by the Unified Co-operative Service to train union personnel, although it will take some time before the system is fully operational.

With regard to the education of committee-men, the problem of efficiency, in terms of educational investment and output, is that, due to the democratic nature of co-operatives, no system has yet been devised which would ensure that the committee would stay in office until they had fully or satisfactorily served the societies to the extent of the educational investment. This situation is further aggravated by the risks of electing potentially unqualified committee-men. At the previous CUT meetings, it has been recommended that the Act should be amended, so that, once a committee is elected, it should remain in office for 5 years along the party and parliamentary lines. This may perhaps offer a partial answer.

The problem of efficiency, as far as member education is concerned, can be viewed by comparing the investment made in finalising the superstructures for carrying out member education effectively. Although equipment, funds and personnel are constantly employed, on account of the great distances of members from one another, it becomes difficult to organise them so as to fully utilise the capacities of the educational effort. It is for this reason that we are looking hopefully to the establishment of *Ujamaa* villages. In these villages, it will be easier to reach the farmer!

Brown Ngwilulupi

The Co-operative Union of Tanganyika

Q. Mr. Ngwilulupi, co-operation is an important aspect of economic development in a socialist country. It is the only sensible means whereby the ordinary man can put at least his cent and shilling at the disposal of the development of his country. Your work therefore is of great interest to the ordinary people of our Republic. Could we begin by asking you to give our readers a brief history of the co-operative movement in the country?

A. There have always been, and there are numerous instances in the history of Tanzanian society in which the principles of the traditional extended family system, with its emphasis on co-operation and self-respect and responsibility, were practised.

Individuals or groups of people have from time immemorial come together to achieve certain aims in co-operation with others. In all tribal societies people cultivated their land together, grazed their cattle together, built their houses together, and even defended the principles for which they stood together, when they were challenged by forces outside the tribal circles. In fact co-operation has been the order of the day in all Tanzanian communities.

However, organized co-operatives, as we know them today, came into being in 1932 with the enactment of the first Co-operative Societies Ordinance. The first 12 co-operatives to be registered were in Kilimanjaro. The movement then spread very rapidly throughout the eastern, southern and western parts of Tanzania and by the end of 1961 there were 857 societies.

Brown Ngwilulupi is the Secretary-General of the Co-operative Union of Tanganyika. The following two interviews were originally published in *The Nationalist* for June 3 and 4, 1971. They are reprinted by kind permission.

After Independence, the movement spread like fire and many co-operatives were organized in vast sections of the country with the aim of the indigenous people controlling the economy of our independent country.

Thus great strides have been achieved towards this expansion. The number of societies has increased from 12 in 1932 to 857 in 1961 and 1 533 at the end of April, 1966 to more than 1 700 this year.

Q. Do you attribute early lack of rapid progress in the co-operative movement to imperialist fear of allowing the African to enter the economic field?

A. As I pointed out to you above, it is not true that progress has been slow in the co-operative movement in Tanzania. Nevertheless, we believe the colonial government, just like any other imperialist government, was interested in the organisation of co-operative associations which would facilitate easier channelling of Tanzanian agricultural produce to feed its industries at home—hence the springing up of many marketing co-operatives of farmers which the colonial government branded as "the best form of economic organisation for Tanganyika."

But with Tanganyika's transition to Independence, and subsequent advance to Republican status, new forms of co-operative enterprises have emerged in the fields of savings and credit, wholesale and retail distribution, transport, small-scale industries, consumer co-operation and what have you.

Q. What would you say has been the impact on the development of the country of the co-operative movement?

A. Co-operatives are forces which help in breaking the circle of poverty on the land by helping the farmers and workers to organize themselves collectively to improve production, enjoy better yields and thus provide not only domestic savings for economic expansion but also national enthusiasm for development and mass participation without which the building of *Ujamaa* is impossible. The co-operative movement has therefore enabled the farmer to take his proper place in the national economy. It has shown the nation what can be done by unity, allied to the efficiency and justice implicit in the philosophy underlying all co-operatives.

It has been a school for democracy in which some of the Tanzanian leaders of today received their training in leadership.

Its societies are spearheads in the war against poverty, ignorance and disease, pledged to make independence an economic reality by giving fair incentives for hard work, as stipulated in the Arusha Declaration.

Co-operation has harnessed the combined energies of a rapidly growing number of farmers to feed, clothe, house and transport themselves better, educate themselves and their children, improve their agriculture, process their own crops, build their own hotels, provide their own libraries and newspapers and generally better their economic and social life. Co-operation has thus striven to encourage better farming, better business and better living.

These developments have broadened the base of the movement, which is expected to embrace all important sectors of the national economy in which people can and should participate closely through their own self-governing and self-responsible co-operative organisations.

Q. In official notes issued by your office, it is stated that major development in co-operation followed *uhuru* (independence) in December 1961, since which date the number of registered societies has almost trebled, with 1 670 societies on the register as at the 30th June, 1969. What is your target as at the end of the current Five-Year Development Plan?

A. A co-operative is a free association of persons legally constituted for the purpose of conducting an economic enterprise or business which they control and administer democratically, according to established principles and techniques, to further their own well-being and the well-being of the society.

You will, therefore, see that this definition embodies the four main principles of co-operation:

(*a*) The association is of human beings as such and not of capital;

(*b*) The members of the association are equal, the accepted rule being "one member—one vote";

(*c*) The act of association is voluntary;

(*d*) The association has objectives in which the members have a common interest, and the attainment of which requires the contribution of each.

From this explanation, you will, I hope, be able to deduce the fact that it is not for us (Co-operative Union of Tanganyika Limited) or the Government, for that matter, to have a target of the number of co-operatives we shall have at the end of 1974. The decision to form any co-operative will stem from the farmers themselves when they feel by doing so, they will be able to pool their resources together to eradicate their socio-economic problems. Thus formation of co-operatives cannot be imposed from above. It stems from the grassroots.

But—since you have mentioned the Second Five Year Plan—you must have probably noted that in the Plan it is clearly stipulated that emphasis has been centred on making efficient the marketing functions of co-operatives, while advocating new growth in the direction of production and multipurpose primary societies, and at the same time encouraging the existing societies to provide services to *Ujamaa* communities as they develop.

Chicken-meat Importation

Q. Mr. Ngwilulupi, while there are a lot of oranges in Muheza, a lot of chicken in Dodoma, and people can be encouraged to keep more chickens for the hotel tables and for places like Mwadui, one still eats foreign chickens and foreign fruits in our hotels. What is the co-operative movement doing about this aspect of development?

A. According to figures available, Tanzania is nearing self-sufficiency as far as importation of chicken meat is concerned. For instance, in 1967 the value of imported chicken meat was Shs. 1 023 920: in 1968 this dropped to Shs. 813 300 and in 1969 to Shs. 435 866. Last year the value of imported chicken meat was Shs. 110 191. From those figures you will note that we are almost self-sufficient in this commodity.

As for fruit-canning, the capital involved to set up secondary industries is very large indeed. Fruits are seasonal, very highly perishable crops. In order to have an economically viable fruit-canning industry, a lot of cold-storage facilities are needed to enable the factory to operate in full swing the whole year.

Again, although it might appear on the face value that many farmers in Muheza, Njombe, Kyela, Tabora, etc. grow a considerable amount of fruit, most of them are doing this on an individual basis. As I said earlier, our aim in the movement is not to encourage individual small-scale capitalists but to encourage co-operative farming units among our members at primary level.

I would therefore think that, should these farmers in the said areas decide to work together in *Ujamaa* villages, it would facilitate a concerted effort on the part of the movement, the National Milling Corporation and the National Agricultural Food Corporation to establish small processing plants for their fruits, as is being done for crops like cotton, coffee and what have you.

Q. Since this country has embarked upon *Ujamaa* as its goal, do you not think that the time has now come when co-operation must be seriously taught as a subject in schools?

A. Possibly you are aware that *Ujamaa* villages and co-operative societies are identical, in that their literal meanings are the same. To talk of *Ujamaa* as being different from *ushirika* (co-operation) and vice versa is indeed absurd, for these are part and parcel.

However, a provision is made in school syllabi for the teaching of co-operation. At present, arrangements are under way here at the Co-operative Union of Tanganyika Limited to conduct school broadcasts on co-operation for primary-school children and this will spread to secondary schools too.

In all regions we now have co-operative-education teachers, who are actively engaged in teaching co-operation to farmers. These are also utilized in teaching co-operation to schools. Recently a circular letter was sent by the CUT to all heads of secondary schools, that they should make use of these teachers, who are available on request. The response from headmasters of secondary schools has been very encouraging indeed.

Q. Mr Ngwilulupi, the Second Development Plan places great emphasis on the expansion of co-operative activity in matters of rural development. Apart from steps to increase the strength of co-operative development to 1 072 officers and inspectors by 1973/75, what is the CUT doing to stimulate and consolidate co-operation in *Ujamaa* villages?

A. I told you earlier that one cannot talk of co-operative societies and *Ujamaa* villages as being distinct. It is only a problem of semantics and we would like you to drive home this fact to all your readers.

Ujamaa villages are rural co-operative villages and the intention of the *Ujamaa* villages policy is to introduce the concept of the small groups in a village co-operating as a family for the communal good of all. This is a conscious attempt to move away from the concept of the individual peasant producers adopting the incentives and ethics of a capitalistic system, and to move away from the principle of personal gain towards the principle of mutual gain. In forming such co-operative villages, alias *Ujamaa* villages, there is no element of compulsion or coercion. Adoption of the idea is left to the people themselves and to their own initiative.

However, the CUT role is to provide leadership by educating the masses. We are now actively engaged in the promotion of *Ujamaa* villages through our co-operative teachers in the field. Their work necessitates talking, discussing, explaining and persuading the people by actions to show what we are urging them to do.

At present most of the requirement of the *Ujamaa* villages, like fertilizers, insecticides, etc., are channelled to these villages through the already established co-operatives. Again the unions have been asked by the CUT to assist *Ujamaa* villagers financially when their crops are not yet ready, to prevent the current trend of villagers abandoning their village for 2–3 months to work for capitalistic large shamba owners. The most significant role of course is for the co-operatives to provide marketing services and other facilities to the *Ujamaa* villages.

Nevertheless, there is no limit to what all of us can do in order to encourage the formation of *Ujamaa* villages. But this is a national task and not only of the co-operative movement. TANU is leading in this.

Q. How many co-operative societies have in fact been organised by the CUT in the *Ujamaa* villages so far established in the country?

A. I think my answer to question 8 will answer this question as well. My emphasis was that the ultimate stage of the organisation of *Ujamaa* villages is to have production, multi-purpose co-operative societies, which are the highest form of co-operation. You will, therefore, agree with me that the best way is to transform the present societies performing the sole role of marketing into societies which will perform other functions.

As such, many of the old societies have already started providing other services, e.g. distribution of the basic needs of life (consumer co-operatives), savings and credit facilities, etc. Our role is not to establish co-operative societies within other co-operative societies, i.e. the *Ujamaa* villages, but to transform the existing co-operatives into multi-purpose production-oriented societies, while at the same time rendering essential services to the *Ujamaa* villages established as separate entities.

Q. Listening to one TANU Political Education Officer at a TAPA seminar the other day, I was impressed by his statement that what Tanzania needs today is not *washawishi* (advisers) but *watendaji* (executing officers). In what way do you think the officers employed in this Plan period will be executing officers working with the peasants to create more revolutionary and progressive co-operative societies rather than pen-pushers and advisers?

A. Your question does not seem to be clear. You are probably taking it for granted that all officers employed within the co-operative movement, for whom I speak, are pen-pushers. This is a very wrong attitude. In fact all of them are executing officers, in that their roles today are those of executives.

Gone are the days when co-operative personnel were being used as advisers. They used to advise the farmers on how to form co-operatives. Now they are working hand in hand with peasants in their respective co-operative societies to show them by actions what it is that they are urging the farmers to do. To achieve this end, there is very good collaboration between the movement's staff and the extension officers employed by Kilimo.

But one thing that you have to take into consideration is the fact that co-operatives are business organisations. In order to work efficiently, there must be a demarcation of duties. You cannot expect 100 employees of a co-operative to go into the field all at one time. There must be people who plan, look after the books, distribute fertilizer and insecticides, etc. This kind of demarcation is commonplace.

Q. Would you not say that these co-operative officers could also become administrative secretaries of the co-operative societies, in the same way, as the Regional Commissioner or the Area Commissioner is a Regional Secretary or District Secretary, respectively, of TANU? Do you not think that this system would save the co-operatives money, as well as bring the officers closer to the day-to-day problems of the co-operative movement?

A. Perhaps you need clarification on the structure of co-operative personnel before I even try to answer your question. On the one hand, we have the co-operative-movement personnel working in the societies and unions closely with the farmers. On the other hand, there are Government personnel under the Registrar of Co-operatives whose main roles are those of auditing, supervision and making sure that the performance of co-operatives is within the law.

Now, coming back to your question, you remember I told you earlier that co-operatives are democratic institutions, whose affairs are handled by the owners and users of the services provided by co-operatives—the members. Through delegation, the members vest their powers of employing and accepting employees to the managing committees of the co-operatives. Once appointed, these employees become the administrative secretaries of their societies. The societies, in turn, affiliate themselves to a regional union, whose chief executive officer is a manager.

The manager is therefore an administrative officer, as far as the societies affiliated to his union are concerned. On the other hand, he works very closely with the Government co-operative officers mentioned above, in seeing that the social and economic aspects of the co-operatives in that particular region are upheld accordingly. I cannot therefore envisage the need for other administrative secretaries, now or in the future, other than the ones we already have in the movement.

Q. In what way has the setting of the Unified Co-operative Service helped to bring about more reliable and dedicated co-operative service personnel?

A. Success or failure of a co-operative is closely linked with the character and ability of management. The reason most frequently stated for failure among co-operatives is "inefficient management". This is not surprising, because from a broad point of view management is concerned with planning, organising, and staffing key personnel, direction and leadership, and co-ordinating and controlling all of the activities of the co-operative.

Briefly stated, management deals with all the varied activities of a co-operative, such as member relations, financing, handling members' products, pooling sales returns, purchasing supplies, merchandising, transportation, maintaining satisfactory accounting and other necessary records and numerous other phases of the co-operative's operations. It is readily seen why "inefficient management" is the dominant reason given when a co-operative fails.

So you can see the running of a co-operative is not a job for an amateur. Since all co-operatives are businesses, they should be operated by people who are trained for their jobs. Now to attract the best type of employees, there should be opportunity for advancement as a man gains experience and status, and in the context of the co-operative movement in Tanzania this implies access to other societies and unions. This has been the function of the Unified Co-operative Service since its inception.

Again, the engagement, discipline, terms of service, and dismissal of secondary and national co-operative employees, which was under the legal control of the committees, has been vested with the United Co-operative Service. Apart from the fact that this has consequently obliterated nepotism, it has also helped to cultivate confidence and enhance employees' performance from the support they receive from such a central organisation.

Q. Mr. Ngwilulupi, the President declared 1970 as well as 1971 as years of adult education. What practical plans have you for the intensification of adult education this year? What plans have you for the future?

A. Adult education is considered as an integral part of the business development of each Tanzanian co-operative. We in the co-operative movement believe that, in the long run, people make progress only through education. But the economic problems of life are the most urgent and pressing for the great majority of our people, and therefore participation in co-operatives gives substance and realism to education for the masses. Thus, in our mind, adult education and co-operation become the true instruments of social progress for the people. Adult education in the co-operative societies in Tanzania caters for three groups of people—the members, the committee-men, and the staff.

Members

At present many farmers utilize the marketing co-operatives without being members. A membership campaign launched last year has been carried on well into 1971. The ultimate aim is to enrol all farmers as members.

Produce marketing, *Ujamaa* villages, and membership in co-operative societies, etc. are subjects taught at day-long courses all over the country which are attended by the farmers.

Committee-men

Courses, the duration of which varies from one to several weeks, are conducted by over 50 co-operative-education teachers spread all over the country to the more than 17 000 committee-men in our co-operatives.

The Co-operative Union's Education Department in Moshi has produced over seven correspondence courses, which are being studied by the committee-men as well as other farmers.

The correspondence courses are supplemented by radio programmes every week. Correspondence courses can be studied individually or in study groups. The idea is that each primary society should have a permanent study group which meets regularly, at least once a fortnight, and consists of the secretary, 3–4 committee-men and some members, about 15 people in all. At present there are over 1 200 such groups operating in the country.

Staff

The Co-operative College in Moshi conducts various courses for both the movement and Government staff—on all levels, including staff for *Ujamaa* villages.

So, you can see that co-operative education in Tanzania is a well-thought-out system, whereby an ordinary citizen who becomes interested and involved in the co-operative movement as a member can move from one stage to another within the system. The current enrolment is over 40 000. There are about 10 000 people taking correspondence courses. Over 2 000 staff members are being trained and 1 000 committee-men.

This makes co-operative education one of the biggest adult-education programmes in Tanzania, with a wide geographical coverage.

The methods of instruction are "adult" and up-to-date. The study-group method, where people meet as equals to learn something by discussing and finding solutions and answers together, has been successfully introduced by the co-operative movement. The combination of group work, correspondence material, film shows and radio programmes, tried out by us, will, I hope, soon be taken up by other adult-education bodies.

We have succeeded remarkably in producing our own study materials and I will not be far from the truth by saying that we are the only major adult-education body which is not very much troubled by shortage of materials and aids. This is indeed a very grand achievement.

Q. One problem which constantly haunts the farmer is the fluctuation of world prices. What is the CUT doing to educate the farmer on this aspect of his occupation as a normal business phenomenon?

A. This question was partly answered above. I said that we have over 50 co-operative teachers throughout the country, whose main function is to organise courses to educate the farmers on the purposes of co-operatives, the principles of the movement and its structure, the rights and responsibilities of members, the way a properly constituted co-operative should function, and the relation of co-operatives to the marketing boards and to the Government.

But my personal opinion is that the problem of price fluctuations is a national one and should not be left to the few teachers we have. Marketing Boards, TANU and Government officials should embark on a campaign to educate the farmer on this important but always problematic matter.

Q. In a number of places in the country it is quite obvious that the farmer is subjected to constant temptation by traders outside the co-operative movement to sell his crop to them rather than to the co-operative society or to a board concerned. What are you doing (*a*) to remove the factors which make the pirates thrive and (*b*) to stamp out completely this type of economic piracy?

A. It is good that you appreciate that the co-operative movement has enemies outside the movement as well as within it, e.g. the private traders and others who lost business to the Co-operatives; some of these enemies have not given up hope of ruining the co-operatives and they use devious tricks to bring about their downfall. In some cases, even leaders were taken as tools by these enemies, to use their influence to harm the interest of this movement.

However, the main factor to be used in trying to alleviate this problem is the farmer himself—though we must admit that it takes time to educate a co-operative member as to his rights and responsibilities, as compared with a non-member who is tempted by profit-seeking traders outside the co-operative.

We do not see any other way of eradicating the economic piracy other than through educating the farmer, to enable him to be more loyal to his co-operative, for, despite the fact that laws have been enacted a long time ago, the pirates are still thriving.

Our other hope is that, as the farmers are politically orientated, they will probably expose the illegal traders to the police and/or other co-operative personnel (and this has been done in some places), for the law to take its course.

Q. The decision by the Government to give, as a step toward eliminating exploitation, the CUT a national monopoly in the distribution of certain basic foodstuffs, such as maize, wheat, flour, rice and sugar, is both timely and praiseworthy. How much business has CUT handled so far and what does this mean in terms of reducing exploitation of the consumer? Is there a danger of the Co-operative Union of Tanganyika Limited taking the place of a wholesale exploiter?

A. It is rather confusing to talk of the CUT as having been given a monopoly in the distribution of certain consumer commodities. In fact, it is Government policy that the distribution business should eventually be placed in the hands of the co-operative movement as a whole and not only of CUT as such.

Thus, almost all the regional co-operative unions are now engaged in distribution activities involving the commodities you have mentioned and many others. The unions are now opening up retail shops in the societies affiliated to them. In this way the *dukawallas* will disappear slowly—as the farmers will eventually get all their basic needs from their co-operatives and they will not have to travel to town to buy anything from these people.

However, as far as *Ugawaji* is concerned, it is a joint venture between CUT and the National Milling Corporation on a 50–50 basis. National Distributors Limited, a result of this joint venture, is responsible for wholesale distribution of the items you have mentioned in Dar es Salaam only.

Goods-hoarding

Initially the idea was to have a National Distribution Company, as the name suggests, to serve up-country co-operatives, but since, as I said before, almost every co-operative union has embarked upon distribution, we have found it fit that the area of operation of National Distributors Limited be limited to Dar es Salaam only.

I think I need not elaborate on the advantages of having such people's tools as National Distributors Limited, for I believe you are quite conversant with them. Since its inception, National Distributors Limited has completely eradicated the constant price fluctuations, which were plaguing Dar es Salaam citizens, including the abolition of hoarding of some essential commodities by capitalistic speculators, and the constant adulteration of goods which was the order of the day in the city.

As far as reducing exploitation is concerned, the mere existence of such peoples' organs acts as a check on price fluctuations. An individual wholesaler will think twice before raising the price of a commodity if he knows a co-operative society or a joint co-operative venture such as National Distributors Limited will be selling the same at a much lower price.

As regards Co-operative Union of Tanganyika Limited taking the place of a wholesale exploiter, I have already explained that CUT does not deal directly in distribution, but does so through investment in National Distributors Limited, which is registered as a company and not as a co-operative.

But I feel obliged to tell you for your information that in the case of a co-operative there is no profit in the sense in which the word is used in business. In business a profit is made by selling goods or services to outside persons at a higher price than the cost of making or purchasing and distributing them.

Consumer Co-operatives

But in a consumer co-operative society members associate to make or purchase and distribute goods for their own use, not to sell to the public. Therefore, when making purchases from the society, if they individually pay more for the goods than it costs to make or purchase and distribute them, there is no profit in the real sense, for a person cannot make a profit out of himself or herself.

If the society sold the goods to its members at cost price, plus expenses, the question of profit would not arise. When the society sells the goods at a higher price than the cost price, plus expenses, and distributes the excess to its members as dividend upon purchases at the end of the trading period, there is no profit, because the dividend upon purchases is in reality a reduction of the price paid by the member.

The net price paid by the member is then the approximate cost, plus expenses. For these reasons the term "surplus" is generally used in co-operative societies instead of the term "profit".

With that explanation the CUT would never have taken the place of a wholesale exploiter, were it directly engaged in wholesale distribution.

Q. In what way do you think the existence of the Co-operative Union of Tanganyika Limited is conducive practically to the development of the co-operative movement in the country?

A. The Co-operative Union of Tanganyika Limited is an essential unifying entity of the co-operative movement. It has a very great potential as an influence to consolidate present development and future progress. It has the major role of speaking for the movement as a whole within Tanzania and in international circles.

Apart from the fact that the co-operative movement in Tanzania is developing to a point where it is becoming increasingly involved in agricultural processing factories, financing of large-scale operations, wholesale distribution, large-scale development skills, knowledge and attitudes within the hierarchy in the movement, etc., it is felt that no single primary co-operative society or regional union is capable of meeting these demands and others successfully if they are not united together.

It is for this reason, therefore, that an adequate structure has been set up to deal with problems which one co-operative institution cannot solve alone—hence the formation of the Legal Department, the Co-operative Education Centre, which is the Education Department of CUT, the Ushirika Newspaper Department, and the Insurance Department, all of which serve all unions.

In the near future it is intended to set up other departments to provide essential services to all unions, but the establishment of these departments will, of course, depend on the needs of the unions as they develop and the finances available.

Stumbling-blocks

Q. Back to co-operative societies. Why is it that consumer co-operative action to date has been almost exclusively concentrated on urban development? Do you not think that it is a vital aspect of co-operation to remove exploiters particularly in *Ujamaa* villages?

A. Efforts to establish consumer co-operatives in urban as well as rural areas in Tanzania go back many years. It is not true that these efforts have exclusively been confined to urban areas only. In fact, today in Tanzania there are many more consumer co-operatives in the rural areas than in towns.

But, as I said earlier, co-operatives uphold the principle that the decision to start a co-operative, be it consumer or marketing, should always stem from the masses, as they are the ones who feel the need and will ultimately use its services. It is wrong to impose this decision from above. Past instances have proved that doing so would be detrimental to any society formed in that way.

Consequently, efforts are being made at both Co-operative Union of Tanganyika Limited, regional unions and the societies to mobilise the masses so that they form their own consumer societies in both urban and rural areas.

However, the establishment of a consumer shop is not without its setbacks. Lack of capital, lack of trained people, acute competition from private shop-owners, disloyal membership and what have you have always been stumbling blocks to the achievement of this goal.

To counteract the problem of skilled personnel, a comprehensive training programme for consumer co-operative personnel is run at the Co-operative College, Moshi. A model consumer shop at the College is used as a training ground for these personnel.

Retail Trade

And as I told you earlier, marketing co-operative societies are slowly but surely being engaged in retail trade under closely controlled conditions by the distribution wings of the regional unions to which these societies are affiliated. We hope when this undertaking has spread to all the societies, another chapter will have been opened in the history of the co-operative movement in Tanzania, for we shall have been able to provide to the farmers a reliable source of staple merchandise at a price which reflects their combined purchasing power.

Q. Why is it that, of the 1 670 co-operative societies registered in 1969, only eight were of fishermen, when there is a lot of fish in the country and fishermen are prone to exploitation?

A. To organize fishermen into co-operatives is not an easy task at all. This is because the fishing canoes used for fishing are, more often than not, owned by capitalists. The only solution to this problem would be for the fishermen to organise themselves into *Ujamaa* villages. In this way, their efforts could be supplemented by assistance from the regional unions as well as the Government.

To set up a viable fishing industry is an expensive endeavour. A lot of cold-storage facilities as well as costly processing plants will definitely be needed—at the outset. An *Ujamaa* village would therefore probably be the answer to this problem.

Co-operative Laws

However, fish being a highly perishable product, the development of the industry, as envisaged in the Second Five-Year Development Plan, will require a carefully co-ordinated expansion of production, processing and marketing facilities. In the Plan, it is therefore proposed to establish experimental *Ujamaa* village fishing at Moa, Bagamoyo, Pangani, Mafia, Kilwa and Lindi. We hope that, if these are successful, they will spread to all areas in the country where there is good potential for fishing.

Q. Mr Ngwilulupi, what is the relationship of the CUT with such parastatal organisations as Intrata, the National Development Corporation and the State Trading Corporation?

A. I think that you know very well that the relationship is one of mutual understanding, in that the aim of all the institutions you have mentioned, including CUT, is to enable the workers and farmers to reap the benefits and fruits of a socially, politically and economically independent Tanzania—where the dignity of man is upheld uppermost in our minds, while the exploitation of man by man is condemned to its roots.

Q. Do you think the time has come when the co-operative laws of the country should be changed in order to imbibe the ideas gained as a result of the establishment of *Ujamaa* villages?

A. For your information, the Managing Committee of the Co-operative Union of Tanganyika Limited appointed a sub-committee recently to look into this matter—since the greatest task of the co-operatives now is to assist in the implementation of the country's policy of *Ujamaa* villages, by forming production-based multi-purpose societies and by orientating marketing-based societies towards the establishment of farming units.

We feel, therefore, that the time has come when some changes should be made in the current by-laws of co-operatives as well as in the ordinances and rules to incorporate these new ideas. This was the endeavour of the said CUT sub-committee and its findings and recommendations will be disclosed when all concerned have had an opportunity to scrutinize them.

Q. What is your relationship with external co-operative movements? In what way are these subsidizing or assisting your activities or those of your affiliated societies?

A. The Co-operative Union of Tanganyika Limited is a full-fledged member of the International Co-operative Alliance—which is a world-wide body comprising associations of national unions of co-operative societies, which seek to promote a non-profit system of production and trade, organised in the interests of the whole community and based upon voluntary and mutual self-help.

ICA Membership

The purpose of the International Co-operative Alliance is to propagate co-operative principles and methods and to promote friendly and economic relations between co-operative organisations of all types, both nationally and internationally.

From the above you will notice that the International Co-operative Alliance does not in any way subsidize or assist the activities of the Co-operative Union of Tanganyika Limited or those of the unions and societies affiliated to CUT.

Q. A personal question. How did you get interested and involved in the co-operative movement, Mr. Ngwilulupi?

A. Well, I started like any other person, and through hard work and devotion to duty, I rose up the ladder—just like you did.

Co-operatives in Uganda

A Paper Presented by the Department for Co-operative Development, Uganda

Authorities on management differ widely on the definition of management. It will suffice to say that management in its broadest sense will include the process of effective planning, organisation, direction and control of an undertaking so as to achieve the desired goals.

Efficiency may be described as the execution of a project in the minimum time but with the maximum benefits. In Uganda, efficiency in co-operative management involves primary societies, district co-operative unions and apex co-operative organisations. It covers matters like manpower (its availability, recruitment, training, promotion, and welfare), finance (its source, use and especially scarcity), and various systems of control designed to suit particular situations. In brief, the subject is so extensive that it will be necessary to confine this paper to a limited range of problems which can usefully be discussed at some length. In this context, it is intended to devote more time to finance and manpower.

Social and Economic Background

Like most developing countries in Africa and elsewhere, Uganda is predominantly an agricultural country. The backbone of its economy is the peasant farmers. Their livelihood is derived from income obtained from crops grown for home consumption and the sale of cash crops (mostly coffee and cotton) which are exported abroad. Coffee, which is by far the greatest source of foreign exchange, is facing severe competition from overseas. This commodity is already in abundant supply on the world markets and is subject to quota restrictions imposed by the International Coffee Organisation, of which Uganda is a member. Prices are characteristically unstable and on a downward trend. Cotton, which ranks second as an earner of foreign exchange, does not suffer to the same extent as coffee from the problem of over-production, although generally prices are on a downward trend, owing to severe competition from man-made fibres.

It will now be apparent that, if the country is to reap the greatest financial benefit from its two major export crops on the competitive world market, it will be necessary to offer for sale the best quality products at minimum cost. This, of course, does not occur by accident. It needs plenty of effort, and involves the farmers, the co-operatives, the marketing boards and the government in planning and executing the plans. All are important.

Uganda's co-operatives have a big part to play in the economic development of the country. Co-operatives market and process all the dry-processed coffee produced in the country. This accounts for about 80% of the coffee crop. In addition, the entire cotton crop is bought, ginned and locally marketed by co-operatives, although, where ginning capacity is inadequate, co-operatives gin their cotton on contract in privately owned ginneries. Such cases are negligible. Besides, co-operatives market locally a variety of other produce, for example, groundnuts, maize and millet, but the amounts involved are not yet very large. It may be mentioned that, because of the need to diversify the country's economy, in order to reduce over-dependence on coffee and cotton, the co-operatives, like private individuals and companies, are now involved in the marketing of milk and have gone into ranching. Co-operatives are also, with some difficulty, engaging in the distribution business through consumer shops and agricultural supply shops. Initial steps have been taken to involve co-operatives in the insurance business. The newly re-activated Uganda Co-operative Development Bank Ltd. is now doing good business.

It may also be mentioned that the price structure for crops in the country is government-controlled. Coffee and cotton prices to the farmer are fixed by the Government and minimum prices in the case of some other crops are also fixed. Prices to processors are also fixed in the cases of cotton and coffee. So the final return to the co-operatives, at least for the major crops, is limited and is dependent on the margins of profit allowed. Efficiency is therefore of supreme importance. But how does one measure efficiency in co-operatives? Possibly by comparing similar types. At the end of 1970 in Uganda there were 2 238 registered societies, including 36 unions and apex organisations, plus several unregistered groups. The membership of primary societies was nearly 650 000 families. The combined turnover of the movement was Shillings (Uganda) 800 million, broken down as follows:

	Millions of Ugandan Shillings
Coffee	4.80
Cotton	2.90
Groundnuts, Maize, Millet, Other Commodities	3.01

It is against this background that co-operatives in Uganda have to measure and examine their efficiency.

Efficiency in Financial Management

(*a*) *Sources of capital.* In this highly competitive world, no worthwhile development is possible without a reasonable supply of capital. One of the great ills of the developing countries is the severe shortage of capital. Uganda is no exception to this. In this country the traditional sources of capital for the co-operative movement are as follows:

Share capital, which forms a very small proportion of the movement's capital.

Reserve funds, which form the largest percentage (the movement's own capital).

Deposits from members on a short-term basis, which are also negligible in amount.

Loans from commercial banks, mostly bank overdrafts for operating capital, largely for buying and processing produce. These are invariably short-term.

Loans from the Government are practically all long-term. These are loans made to co-operative unions or apex organisations to acquire or build coffee factories and ginneries. Such funds are channelled through the Uganda Commercial Bank.

The Government has also provided short-term loans to societies for re-lending to farmers who are members of societies for the improvement of their farms.

World Bank and other external loans. These are very few indeed and are a recent innovation, mostly in connection with the Beef Ranching and the Small-holders' Tobacco Projects.

(*b*) *Characteristics of co-operative capital.* It will be seen that the capital available to co-operatives has the following main characteristics. First, practically all long-term capital and an overwhelming proportion of the short-term capital is *borrowed* money. This is inevitably expensive capital. Secondly, by far the greater part of the co-operatives' own funds is made up of reserves. This is cheap capital.

(*c*) *Possible new sources of capital.* Because the profit margins of co-operatives are comparatively small and the cost of borrowed capital prohibitive, a new move was initiated this year by the Department for Co-operative Development to obtain cheap capital for long-term developments. In the past, the practice has been for co-operatives, whenever they made a surplus, to follow members' wishes and distribute all the surplus (less the statutory allocation to the reserve fund etc.) back to its members in the form of bonus. Although there were various pressures in favour of this practice, some political, it must be said this was possibly not the best kind of financial management.

The new development is now to encourage, indeed, almost to insist that societies and unions capitalise an appreciable proportion of their bonus, say, 50%, which is turned into loan capital. This is repayable as and when liquid funds are available and carries a low interest rate of, say, 4% per annum. In commercial language, this may be termed "undated stock". This arrangement ensures that co-operatives can carry out the much-needed rehabilitation of factories and ginneries and start new ventures, without resorting to expensive and often difficult-to-get outside capital.

(*d*) *Management of capital.* It has been established in the foregoing paragraphs that co-operatives, through force of circumstances, use expensive capital. It is therefore of the greatest importance that such capital is used efficiently, so as to reap the maximum benefit from it. How can this be done? First, priority must be given to investing any surplus funds in productive ventures. In the case of co-operatives owning factories and ginneries, this means using such funds to effect much-needed improvements in process equipment and storage facilities. This will result in the speedier handling of produce, greater throughput per hour and quicker sales, thus minimising the period for which expensive bank-overdraft facilities are required. In addition, it is known that in the tropics most crops do not keep for long periods unless they are in good storage, which is expensive to construct. So, by speedy handling and processing of crops, the quality of the crops sold by the co-operatives can be appreciably improved with a resultant increase in the price of the crop directly through premiums or indirectly through the avoidance of penalties from the statutory Marketing Boards. On the other hand, a co-operative may decide to invest in a new venture like ranching, a field of development which is indeed very favourable and virtually unlimited in its potentialities.

Perhaps it should be pointed out that in the past mistakes or bad planning have given rise to situations in which the management was handicapped in its efforts to improve efficiency. Cases are known in which, due to sectional pressures within co-operative unions or political pressures from within or outside the unions, excess capacity for ginning cotton was acquired. Such facilities have now become a burden to the management and it cannot be claimed that in such a situation the business can maximise the return on its total investment. However, due to the much-increased vigilance of the Government over the activities of the co-operative movement, such a situation is unlikely to occur again and attempts are being made to correct it.

Besides effecting a sound investment policy as part of efficient management, it is necessary to institute sound accounting systems and financial controls. Because co-operatives have been given a monopoly by the Government to handle most of the country's crops, the few co-operative unions which handle these crops have suddenly become very big and complex businesses. In most cases, the accounting systems designed many years ago to deal with a small volume and range of commodities are now totally unsuitable to cope with this new development. What management desperately needs is a standardized accounting system, which will make financial and other information readily available, so that it can be promptly interpreted and used in the day-to-day running of the business. One additional advantage likely to result from a standardized accounting system, especially for co-operative unions, is that it will now be possible to compare, with some degree of confidence, the performance of one union with that of another, which is rather difficult at present, due to the multiplicity of accounting systems.

In Uganda, there is a great scarcity of qualified accountants. Those who become available are quickly absorbed into private business, statutory boards and other public corporations, which offer bigger salaries than co-operatives.

So, besides the introduction of a standardized accounting system, it would be of tremendous advantage to management if such a system were made as simple as possible, although this must not be at the expense of making the essential information available. Any question of introducing very sophisticated systems must be ruled out in the foreseeable future, simply because the kind of men who take managerial and other decisions are not now, nor will be in the foreseeable future, in a position to appreciate, let alone operate, sophisticated systems. However, the systems proposed will give management information on which to base well-considered decisions, which will promote the efficiency of co-operatives.

Management of Manpower

(a) *Recruitment.* Men in management are a key factor in the efficient running of any business, particularly a public business like a co-operative. Unfortunately for the co-operatives, for various reasons their public image as employers is not as good as it ought to be. The result is that co-operatives—especially co-operative unions and apex organisations—do not always have access to the right type of persons for their vacant posts. Again, sectional interests and political pressures can further confuse the issue, in that, even if a competent person is available, he may not be offered the job for these very reasons. Be that as it may, the Government, through the Co-operative Department, is very much concerned about the need for the unions to be properly staffed. In fact, its concern has become so urgent that the latest Co-operative Societies Act (1970) makes it possible for the Government to appoint and/or remove certain officials of co-operatives, if it sees fit to do so. This power is, of course, a drastic one and is used only in extreme cases of mismanagement or injustice.

It must be pointed out at this stage that, when the co-operatives took over the monopoly of the marketing and processing of the two major crops in the country, there were no qualified Ugandan Africans of any consequence to man this huge business at managerial level—especially the top management. In many instances, Ugandans had to have on-the-job training from expatriate advisors inside the union and from the Co-operative Department through constant advice and supervision.

(*b*) *Training*. The problem of faulty or inadequate recruitment of staff brings us to the next logical step of training. Through training on the job, short and long courses inside and outside the country, seminars and correspondence courses, staff have been found to improve in the performance of their duties. In this context, seminars and courses organised by the Department, the Uganda Co-operative Alliance and the Management Training and Advisory Centre, have contributed much towards equipping co-operative managerial and professional staff with both theoretical and practical knowledge.

The question of training union managerial staff is to be actively pursued when the Co-operative College now under construction is in operation. For technical and professional staff, the movement will continue to rely on the open market.

(*c*) *Retention of staff.* It is generally accepted that continuity of staff is a factor which contributes to the smooth running of the business. Having recruited staff and given some training, where possible, co-operatives must see that they take positive steps to retain such staff. The basic requirement is, of course, to provide terms and conditions of service which are competitive. Unfortunately, this is not always possible, because of the comparatively meagre financial resources available to the co-operatives. As was mentioned earlier, the public image of co-operatives is not as good as it should be. Cases are known in which co-operatives have been used merely as steppingstones to some other employment—including the rise to political power.

In order to increase efficiency at all levels, there is a school of thought which argues that salaries should be modest but that an incentive bonus should be paid to staff as a reward for efficiency. Such a bonus is to be based on pre-determined norms, so that any performance above the norm must attract a bonus. The bonus is to be paid to both production, professional, managerial and other employees. There are two important points to note about these incentive schemes. First, they must be realistic. If the norms are set too high, no one will bother to try to achieve them. Second, they must be fair. If the extra amount to be earned is too small for the extra strain on the potential beneficiaries, again no one will bother much about such an incentive.

It is not the intention here to show that staff recruited by co-operatives—especially co-operative unions, to which most of these remarks relate—are sub-standard. Indeed, many of their employees are outstanding in their respective roles. But the truth is that co-operatives find it more difficult to recruit qualified staff than their counterparts in the private and public sectors.

Final Appraisal

This paper has given the agricultural economic background against which co-operatives operate. They have a monopoly in the marketing and processing of the country's two main export crops—coffee and cotton. It was noted that they operate under virtually predetermined profit margins, which have fluctuated now and again.

Regarding management, two themes have been developed in this paper, namely, financial and manpower management. It has been shown that the sources of finance are very limited, that the proportion of own finance is very low and the movement is heavily dependent on expensive finance, both for short-term and long-term purposes. Such a situation calls for the most efficient use of finance. It has also been shown that problems of manpower are also enormous, but that steps have been or are being taken to make the most efficient use of available manpower.

In conclusion, it can be said that, although there is a lot of room for improvement in the performance of the co-operative movement, it must be accepted that, considering the circumstances under which they operate and the tremendous volume of business which they handle, co-operatives have managed their affairs reasonably well.

M. Lungu

Co-operative Efficiency in Zambia

There has been quite a lot of talk over the past few years about the failings of co-operative societies in Zambia and considerable criticism has been levelled against those charged with the responsibility of organising and establishing these institutions. The greatest fault or failure, so the critics claim, is the inability of the leaders to realise that the movement is failing and to identify those areas which are contributing to the failure and to prescribe the right treatment to cure the disease. Perhaps the critics are right and they may well be correct in their conclusion. But the leaders of the movement, both in the Government and the co-operative societies themselves, have had quite a lot of homework to do. They have now come up with certain suggestions, which, if accepted and acted upon, may well usher in a period of good prospects for a successful co-operative movement.

While it would be useful for the purpose of this discussion to take a close look at the historical background of the development of the co-operative movement in Zambia, it is enough perhaps to say briefly that the period of development can be divided into three parts, firstly, the period between 1914, when the first co-operative society was formed and registered by the Registrar of the High Court, and 1947, when the Department of Co-operative Societies and African Marketing was established. During this period, 10 co-operatives had been formed and they were all predominently white. African participation in the formation of co-operative societies came in 1948, when a new Co-operative Societies Ordinance was

---

M. Lungu is the Senior Co-operative Officer on the National Co-operative Development Committee, Lusaka.

Table 1. *The Development of the Co-operative Movement in Zambia between 1947 and 1964.*

Year	No. of societies registered	Total membership	Share capital* (Kwacha)	Turnover* (Kwacha)
1947[a]	10	1 344	73 000	710 000
1948	37	7 167	200 000	2 290 000
1953	109	16 185	650 078	4 334 638
1958	227	30 003	952 000	9 134 000
1964	212	43 697	1 678 000	11 535 000

[a] These co-operative societies were all European organisations and included such societies as the farmers' co-operatives (just recently abolished), the Co-operative Creameries of Northern Rhodesia (absorbed into the Federal Dairy Board), Zambia Tobacco, the Royal Agricultural Show Society and the Zambesi Dairies.

enacted. Under the Ordinance, the Governor was empowered to appoint a Registrar of Co-operative Societies to exercise the powers attached to the appointment under the Ordinance. The majority of the societies formed between then and 1964 were agricultural marketing societies, through which the African peasant farmers were able to market their surpluses, in order to obtain money to meet their poll-tax payments to the colonial Government. Another type of co-operative society established during this period was the thrift and loan society for urban Africans who were lucky enough to be in regular employment, and the last popular type was the consumer stores, which were also established in urban centres. Both types of co-operative failed. One can only speculate on the reasons for the latter type being organised, as it requires a lot of capital and business know-how. Perhaps it was to save the African from the embarrassment of being served through the hatches in the all-white shops. Table 1 shows the development of the movement between 1947 and 1964.

It is interesting to note the great extent of the contribution made towards the total turnover by these European societies in 1964. One year after the Federation of Rhodesia and Nyasaland came to an end, K7 778 000 of the total turnover

Table 2. *Co-operative Societies as at 31 December 1964.*

	No. of societies	Member-ship	Share capital (Kwacha)	Reserves (Kwacha)	Turnover (Kwacha)
European membership					
Credit	—	—	—	—	—
Consumer & supply	5	2 097	377 262	149 068	2 456 000
Producer marketing	4	287	484 380	289 182	4 357 054
Others	11	1 636	217 324	111 188	965 800
Total European societies	20	4 020	1 078 966	549 438	7 778 854
African membership					
Thrift & credit	38	11 369	410 934	3 672	277 456
Consumer & supply	11	4 512	10 860	16 776	97 480
Producer marketing	126	22 390	65 768	191 024	1 157 196
Secondary	9	174	69 104	438 210	1 418 610
Others	8	1 232	43 222	189 060	805 318
Total African societies	192	39 677	598 888	838 742	3 756 060
Combined totals	212	43 697	1 677 854	1 388 180	11 534 914

was by these European societies, roughly some 63% of the total. One important thing to remember, however, about the European farmers who were members of these societies is that the Land Bank, which was the source of agri-finance, lent money generously to white farmers on very favourable conditions of repayment, which, in certain cases, went up to 30 years.

The next period, and perhaps the most important one which affects us now, is the period from soon after Independence to the present day. The Economic Report for 1966, published by the Ministry of Finance, described the economic conditions pertaining in Zambia in 1965 in the following words:

On the economic side, 1965 was an outstandingly successful year. The gross domestic product (at factor cost) increased by 30% and the gross national income at market prices by 33%. Even allowing for increase in population and rise in many prices, it is clear that real *per caput* national income grew considerably during the year. The monthly average number of persons employed in all industries in Zambia was 28 700 greater than in 1964 and average African earnings for all industries increased by 20%.

It also reported an increase in the urban African population of 44 000 (7%) in 1965.

Such were the boom conditions in Zambia at the time when His Excellency the President made a special appeal to the people to form and organise co-operative societies early in 1965. The call was not without cause. The country had just emerged from the sufferings of colonial domination and economic exploitation as a result of the Federal set-up. After Zambia became a British protectorate and down to the Federal era, development in all spheres tended to favour the white settlers. They had the best educational facilities, the best-paid jobs, better medical services and better houses. They enjoyed all these things in full view of the African population. It is for this reason that, after Independence, the people had great expectations of their first elected Government. The Government was fully aware of these expectations and, to meet them, decided, and very wisely too, to turn to the co-operative movement to carry out its social policy.

The response exceeded all expectations, as hundreds of groups of people were clamouring for registration. The increase in the number of co-operative societies placed a severe strain on the staff of the Department of Co-operative Societies, which, at the end of 1965, totalled only 132, of whom seven were Senior Co-operative Officers. By that time, the number of registered co-operative societies had increased by 123% over the 1964 figures, as Table 2 shows.

As already stated and as can be seen from the figures in Table 2, a great deal of emphasis had been placed on the development of producer marketing. However, after the President's announcement, there was a change in this emphasis, and this made it possible for the co-operative movement to enter into many new fields of economic activity which had hitherto been the prerogative of the white settlers. It is these new fields which have taxed the managerial know-how of a number of co-operative societies' boards of directors, as they came face to face with the realities of the business world. The variety of co-operative societies that were formed included fishing, brick-making, building, farming and farm settlements, and stone-and-sand-supply co-operatives. The Department of Co-operatives was inadequately equipped technically to advise or to adequately supervise the work of most of them, as their numbers had grown out of all proportion to the existing personnel.

But why did the Government decide on co-operatives as a means of carrying out some of its development programme? The answer to this question may be said to have some political overtones, as has already been observed elsewhere in this paper. In deciding on this policy, the following points weighed a great deal in the decision:

(*a*) To meet the people's high expectations following Independence, by involving them physically as much as possible in the economic development of the country.

(*b*) To create viable business organisations which would provide a permanent source of income to as many people as possible, especially those in the rural areas.

(*c*) To form building co-operatives, which would ensure that the First National Development Plan was not delayed or frustrated for lack of staff houses, schools and clinics.

(*d*) To ensure that production co-operatives were established which would open up new areas of production, increase agricultural production and thereby reduce imports.

(*e*) To educate the people in democratic control and to stop the exploitation of one man by another through the application of the co-operative principle of "one man, one vote" and the equitable distribution of profits.

While the movement can claim to have had some measure of success in attaining these objectives, it is also an open secret that many of the co-operatives that were established have since died. It is an accepted fact that the effect of this failure has considerably changed the attitude of many people, more especially of the farming community, towards the co-operative effort in that sector.

As the majority of the co-operative societies which have been formed since are farming co-operatives and settlements and building and brick-making co-operatives, perhaps it will save time to examine these in greater detail, so that we can find out which are the weak areas and the reasons for the poor performance which has marred the image of the co-operative movement in Zambia.

Farming Co-operatives and Settlements

For a very long time, commercial agriculture in Zambia was largely in the hands of white farmers. This European agriculture was not only a source of food and of industrial crops for the Zambian people but was also a large employer of African labour. At Independence, many of these farmers trekked back to Rhodesia or South Africa and it became apparent that the industry would soon collapse unless measures were immediately taken to prevent the situation from deteriorating rapidly. Consequently, the Government introduced several schemes which were aimed at filling the gap in this industry and maintaining agricultural production levels. Such schemes included the introduction of state farms, the establishment of state ranches and the setting up of farming (agricultural) co-operatives and co-operative settlements. These practical schemes were aimed at encouraging the Zambian farmers to move from mainly subsistence production to the cash economy and introducing them to modern mechanised farming. This, of necessity, meant that the Government was prepared to support these schemes with financial assistance in the form of loans, grants and subsidies to ensure a good take-off. One of the subsidy schemes introduced by the Government was the stumping subsidy scheme to farming co-operatives. This encouraged farming co-operatives to stump virgin land for agricultural purposes, by granting each co-operative a K30.00 stumping subsidy for each acre cleared. By the time the scheme was stopped, 49 000 acres of land had been cleared and some K977 000 had been paid out.

Because of this incentive to clear land, many people banded together and hastily settled on any piece of land without first ascertaining its agricultural potential or the accessibility of the markets. Because no definite plans had been made as to how the scheme should operate or be co-ordinated, a somewhat confused situation developed, resulting in failure. For instance, a local political figure—headman or councillor—could urge groups of people to form farming co-operatives, select a very poor piece of land with a few bushes to be uprooted and demand payment of the stumping subsidy. The result was, of course, that many patches of cleared land were scattered all over the country. Some of these were so inaccessible that whatever they might have produced would never have reached the market. Some farms were deserted soon after the members had shared the stumping-subsidy money.

Going hand in hand with this subsidy scheme was the introduction of tractors to speed up agricultural development. These tractors were given to those co-operatives which had 150 acres or more of stumped land. While the mechanisation of agriculture would have definitely had beneficial results, the scheme has not worked according to plan, to say the least. There are many reasons for this:

(*a*) Most of the members who came to form these co-operatives had, for many years, been used to a hoe-and-axe agriculture. The extent of their fields under these conditions was between 2 and 10 acres at most. The demands of big agricultural fields of, say, 300 acres were in certain cases too great for the 10 members. In some societies, it was possible to see members going to the fields at 10 in the morning and "knocking off" at 2 in the afternoon.

(*b*) The introduction of tractors in itself did not help matters. The training of tractor drivers was done hastily and its duration was too short to allow of a better understanding of the machines and their implements. Because of this improper training, tractors were in too many cases not properly maintained and accidents were too frequent, rendering them very unserviceable. It has been reported, for instance, that in one province, where there are 80 co-operative tractors, only

37 are operational. The magnitude of the problem is made worse by the fact that at inception no provision was made for setting up rural workshops to carry out the vital servicing work. It had been hoped to have the tractors attended to by the Mechanical Services Branch of the Ministry of Transport and Power throughout the provinces. But the Mechanical Services workshops were too overcrowded with vehicles to leave the mechanics enough time to attend to these tractors. The attitude of the farmers—that tractors could do everything—also contributed to the fiasco of the tractor scheme.

(*c*) Apart from the local problems which had a direct bearing on agriculture, the Rhodesian Unilateral Declaration of Independence in 1965 also had grave consequences for the operation of the tractor scheme. The fuel, oils, lubricants and spare parts, which normally came through Rhodesia, ceased and the small supplies that there were did not trickle through to the remote parts of the country.

(*d*) The question of agricultural extension services cannot be omitted in this discussion, since a great deal of success in any agricultural activity depends on the efficiency of the extension services. It has already been noted in the case of the Co-operative Department that the staff could not cope with the number of co-operatives that had sprung up. The situation was no better in the Departments of Agriculture and Marketing; in addition to providing the services to co-operatives, they had individuals to attend to as well. Thus, poor crop husbandry was rife in the co-operatives, as most of the members did not know when, what or how to plant. The application of fertilizer, if this was available, was purely guesswork.

(*e*) The establishment of about 800 commercial farming co-operatives was a disincentive.

(*f*) In addition to the already unhealthy state of affairs, the credit with which to purchase requisites such as seed, fertilizer and insecticides was never given on time, so that, when it was provided, co-operative farmers found it impossible to utilize it properly.

(*g*) One cannot avoid mentioning certain universally accepted reasons which have crippled co-operative movements all over the world. They are as follows:

(i) The immaturity of the people.

(ii) The lack of co-operative education.

(iii) Insincerity and corrupt practices by the committees of management.

(iv) The lack of good accounting systems has played a part in the majority of failures in the co-operative movement.

(v) Haste in the formation of most co-operatives in some developing countries.

Of the 805 farming co-operatives that were registered in Zambia, well over 300 have been recommended by the Olund-Russel Report for de-registration, either because they are moribund or have disbanded or are too small and remote to be viable and are therefore useless.

Action to save the farming co-operative movement has been taken on several fronts:

(1) Three hundred and fifty primary co-operative societies have been grouped into 63 unions for the provision of such services as tractor hire, seed and fertilizer distribution, storage and marketing outlets, in addition to the provision of some managerial and book-keeping services. In some areas, the trend now seems to be to form one large farming co-operative instead of a union.

(2) Some farm managers and mechanics have been employed to give the required technical advice and to prepare production programmes. Twenty-one unions have resident farm managers at the moment.

(3) Tractor workshop units have been established at a few union centres to provide maintenance services.

(4) Communal farming, which, for various reasons, has not succeeded, is being replaced by family plots to be worked by an individual, together with his family. The scheme is working well at the Kafubu and Kafulafuta Co-operative resettlement blocks in the Luanshya–Copperbelt Province.

(5) A new Agricultural Finance Company has been set up to administer agricultural credit.

(6) As for marketing, the National Agricultural Marketing Board operates in all the five provinces, except for the

Northern, Southern and Eastern, where co-operative marketing unions are performing this very important service.

(7) Farmer education is being stepped up and co-operative members have been selected to attend short one-week courses at farm institutes run by the Ministry of Rural Development.

It is hoped that, while the agricultural research services are well ahead of practical agriculture in Zambia, the measures outlined above will achieve a measure of success in re-vitalising this very important industry. At present, Zambia is importing heavily to meet its needs of food and food products. The success of any programme lies with the people themselves, if they can apply themselves to the situation. (See Appendix A for a case study of one agricultural co-operative society in the Western Province of Zambia.)

Building and Brick- making Co-operatives

Again, as we have seen in the case of the agricultural industry, the construction sector was dominated by European-owned companies. During the years of the Federation, the bulk of the construction and development capacity was concentrated in Rhodesia. It is estimated that Zambia's capacity during the break-up of the Federation was limited to K30 million, yet, when the Transitional Development Plan was launched, it provided for K54 million worth of construction work, far in excess of its capacity. It became necessary, therefore, to encourage Zambian enterprises to participate and, to this end, 88 building and brick-making co-operatives were established to meet the development targets. Table 3 shows the growth of this sector of the co-operative movement.

As will be noted from the returns in Table 3, the building co-operatives have not reached the construction targets set out in the Development Programme. This lack of absorptive capacity is attributable to a variety of reasons:

(i) While the Government provided the initial capital outlay in the form of loans to purchase vehicles, tools and equipment to the tune of some K2.5 million, the societies themselves

Table 3. *The Growth of the Building and Brick-making Co-operatives in Zambia.*

Year	No. of societies	Member-ship	Share capital (Kwacha)	Reserves (Kwacha)	Turnover (Kwacha)
1965	88	3 729	2 548	—	271 868
1966	92	2 191	5 268	212	760 324
1967	114	2 597	7 506	1 076	1 452 556
1968	143	2 977	7 892	3 468	2 167 644
1969	145	2 076	24 628	4 842	1 368 259
1970[a]	158	4 780	11 873	750	1 441 302

[a] The figures are provisional until verified by the Provincial Officers, and they include sand-supply co-operatives.

failed to generate enough capital of their own to continue efficient operations. The figures for paid-up share capital and built-up reserves in Table 3 speak for themselves.

(ii) A majority of the members of these co-operatives were unskilled labourers, who depended a great deal on the semi-skilled chairman or secretary. It was not unusual to find that only four members out of 43 in a co-operative had the training necessary to build, plaster and roof a building. This situation tended to cause those with the knowledge to exploit their friends. Quarrels would occur and break-away groups became frequent, leaving the co-operative weak and incapable.

(iii) Because of lack of training, most societies were unable to cost building projects, let alone the drawing up of bills of quantity and all that goes with the construction of buildings, making it impossible to work profitably.

(iv) The provision of vehicles by the Government on loan to help in the transportation of building materials to building sites did not solve the problems, as most of these vehicles became the personal properties of chairmen and secretaries, to the disadvantage of the co-operatives.

(v) As in the case of tractors, maintenance became a major problem also with the lorries, as most were operating at a great loss, where no maintenance services were available. Due to the lack of these services, many vehicles have been abandoned for years and have wasted away.

(vi) In most societies, there were no programmes of work. Each member came and left when he felt like it and indiscipline was rampant, all to the detriment of the societies.

These are but a few examples of the bottlenecks that have retarded the progress of building, sand-supply and brick-making co-operatives.

Attempts have been made to correct the situation, both in the agricultural and in the building co-operatives. We have already seen what steps have been taken in respect of the agricultural co-operatives. In the case of the building co-operatives, it was felt that an apex organisation should be established to service these organisations. To this end, the Federation of Building Societies (Co-operatives) was formed in 1968. Some 100 building co-operatives are members of this organisation. Its main tasks are as follows:

(*a*) Ordering and supplying building materials and transporting them to co-operative building sites;

(*b* Preparing and tendering for jobs on behalf of the societies;

(*c*) Offering supervisory services to co-operatives and training the members on the job;

(*d*) Acting as consultant to various building co-operatives.

Since the establishment of this body the situation has not improved very much. This is largely due to staff shortage within the organisation. It is hoped that, once the staff position is satisfactory, the services to the co-operatives will improve and enhance their performance. The target for this organisation is to undertake a building-construction programme of K6 million per annum. They have managed to reach a target of only K2 million. (See Appendix B for a case study of a building co-operative in the Central Province of Zambia.)

To conclude this paper, it is perhaps essential to state here the role of the Co-operative Department itself in the development of the co-operative movement. To many, it would appear that the Co-operative Department is the mother of the movement. This is entirely wrong. Its function is to encourage the people to form co-operatives as a way of achieving economic success for the individual members. It provides the training in business methods and management, and administers the law under which co-operative societies are registered.

In the past, the work of controlling the activities of co-operative societies which were considered to be disregarding their declared aims was rendered difficult because of the limited powers afforded to the Registrar to deal with such situations. A new but comprehensive Act was passed in 1970 to give more powers of control to deal with those co-operatives which did not adhere to co-operative principles. But it is hoped also that the establishment of a National Co-operative Union within a year or so will go a long way towards stabilizing the present situation in the country's co-operative movement.

Appendix A

Case Study of the Shangombo Farming Co-operative Society Ltd, Senanga District, Western Province

This study is based on a tour made by Mr M. Lungu, then Provincial Co-operative Officer, Western Province. Shangombo is but one of the many farming co-operatives whose founders took no notice of the essential economic functions which they are supposed to perform to enable their societies to become viable organisations, offering the members a permanent source of income.

The Shangombo Farming Co-operative was formed and registered in 1968. It comprises 10 members from adjacent villages in the Shangombo area, 147 km from Senanga Boma, an administrative centre in the Western Province of Zambia. It borders on Angola (a Portuguese colony) and is 876 km from Lusaka, the nearest rail terminal.

Just like any other farming co-operative formed during that time, Shangombo Co-operative had cleared a piece of land which was estimated at 15 acres (from my assessment, confirmed by the Provincial Agricultural Officer) but which was officially recorded as 20 acres for the purpose of obtaining a larger slice of the stumping-subsidy cake in accordance with Government policy, as it existed then. The Society had an elected committee of five, which included a chairman, secretary and treasurer, as provided for in the by-laws of the Society. The chairman and the treasurer could not read or write but could speak Lozi, which is widely spoken in the Province, and thus were able to communicate with extension officers who visited them.

At the time of my visit in the company of the Provincial Agricultural Officer (December 4th, 1969) we found four members busy ploughing their field. They had no tractor but they had drought animals and ploughs to till the land with. They had purchased four oxen and two ploughs and two ridgers out of a medium-term loan, provided by the now-defunct Credit Organisation of Zambia, amounting to K2 952. They had also obtained a seasonal loan for the 1969–70 season and part of this money had been earmarked for members' food allowances, while waiting for the crop to grow and be sold. At that point in time, they had ploughed about 20 acres of the field but had not planted anything at all, the reason being that the seed and fertilizer had not been received.

Prior to our leaving for the tour, we had called on the manager of the then Agricultural Rural Marketing Board to find out whether the agricultural requisites, i.e. seed, fertilizer and insecticides, had been despatched to Senanga from Mongu, the provincial headquarters, and had been assured that all was in order. Upon reaching Senanga, we contacted the district supervisor, who took us to the store-rooms, where we found only 21 bags of maize seed, half a bag of bean-seed and eight bags of groundnuts in stock. He informed us that he had despatched some bags across the Zambezi only two days before and he was not sure whether they had reached their destination.

We therefore were not surprised when we were told about the non-arrival of the seed and fertilizer shipment. In any case, the consignment was too small to go round. At that stage, it was a foregone conclusion that the planting would never take place, as the latest date for planting maize stipulated in the instructions of the Department of Agriculture is 15th December of each year, if the crop is to yield anything at all.

The four members stopped ploughing, as we had arrived at about 4 p.m. and they were to knock off anyway. They came to where the others had gathered, just outside the chairman's newly built hut. The members had all moved to live next to their communal farm.

Answering several questions we had asked, it transpired that the last time they had seen their Co-operative Officer was in June 1969 and the District Agricultural Officer in February of that year. The Co-operative Farm Manager had been there in October and had not been seen since then. Next to us was a foodstall containing maize of the 1968–9 harvest, shelled and becoming weevilled. Asked why the maize could not be bagged and sold during the marketing period, we were told that they could not accept the price of K2.00/bag, when they could obtain K4.05 if they sold the maize in Senanga Boma. The estimated number of bags of 200 lbs from that bin would have been 40 and at K2/bag it would only bring in K80.00. This was far below their expectations and they could not accept it. Asked how they proposed to dispose of it, since for each day that passed, the maize would deteriorate further, they said that they hoped to hire a tractor from a neighbouring brick-making co-operative of the same name to transport the maize to Senanga Boma, where it was thought that the price of K4.05 would be paid.

In the backyard of the chairman's hut were some seven packets of fertilizer, carried over from the 1968–9 growing season. Because of poor storage, these appeared to have decomposed and the chairman indicated that 12 were delivered and that five had been used.

Asked about books of accounts, the chairman quickly took out a file containing letters, invoices and blank sheets and said that that was all there was. The secretary was unfortunately away at a relative's funeral.

We took the opportunity to look at the field. The Provincial Agricultural Officer, who had worked for a long time on soil sampling, layout, etc., noticed that the middle of the farm tended to be waterlogged and pointed out that any crop from there would be of poor quality. The soil was sandy and therefore not good for maize production.

The local people usually had cassava as their main food and did not bother to buy or barter for maize. When the members were advised to consume the maize and thus cut down on the money allocated for subsistence, they vehemently rejected the idea.

On my return to Mongu, our resident station, I took my District Co-operative Officer to task regarding this and many similar cases of this nature which seemed to have permeated through the entire system.

Appendix B

Case Study of the Mumbwa Building Co-operative

The Co-operative was founded in early 1966, largely by persons from Rhodesia who had settled in Mumbwa District in the early 1960's. All but one of the original members have left and the present members, with this one exception, do not come from Mumbwa District but from the Northern and Eastern Provinces.

Leadership

(*a*) *Chairman.* A bricklayer who does not hold a trade-test certificate. In February 1970 he decamped with the funds of the Co-operative (around K5 000), with which he purchased a car, a suite of furniture and a new wife.

(*b*) *Vice-Chairman.* He is a trainee bricklayer with Grade 7 education.

(*c*) *Treasurer.* He is a very old man with no training in accounts. He does not have the books of the Society, nor does he know where they are. He says that the chairman was really responsible for the accounts. He is a bricklayer with many years' experience in Rhodesia and has Grade 4 education.

(*d*) *Secretary.* A man with Form 1 education.

Membership

The other members consist of one carpenter and five trainee bricklayers, i.e. the latter were untrained when they joined the Society but are presumably picking up skills as they go along, mainly by working with skilled non-members.

Other Labour

On its present contracts, 32 non-members have been employed, compared with the eight members who have been present for most of the time. The non-members consist of a plumber, four painters, two carpenters, seven bricklayers and 18 labourers.

According to the treasurer, the non-members are paid K7.20 per week for the skilled artisans and K5.40 per week for the unskilled labourers. This amounts to 70% of the *minimum* industrial rates for the building industry.

Equipment

The equipment consists of a cement mixer, which appears to be working, and a lorry, which was purchased in 1966 but which has been out of action since the end of 1967. In fact, it was impounded by the police at that time for being driven in a dangerous condition. Since the Co-operative was unable to pay the fine at the time (maximum K100), the lorry has remained in police storage ever since. According to the treasurer, the police charge 50 ngwee per day for storage fees, so the bill for storage to date amounts to K460. The driver of the lorry was paid on a strange basis: K16 for each trip he made to Kabwe and back—a distance of 200 miles.

Finance

The Co-operative owes K17 000 to the Federation of Building Societies, K3 000 in wages to non-members, who have not been paid for the last three months, and an unknown amount to its members, who have also not received any payments during the same period.

As a result of this non-payment, both members and non-members are on strike. The Co-operative is due to get K14 000 as final payments on two recently completed contracts and K12 000 when it finishes the contract it is at present engaged upon. Apparently this contract could be completed within a month, provided proper supervision were given.

Discipline

Discipline is exercised by the committee, which has power to suspend and to dismiss a member if he continues to be troublesome.

Internal disputes are mainly caused by problems of work-sharing. It is obvious that there have been many disputes in the past, as three former chairmen have left the Co-operative and all but one of the original members have gone. In addition, the only person who knew anything about building plans and the setting-out of buildings left last November.

Supervision

The chairman of the Co-operative is responsible for supervising the work, and he has been responsible in the past for ordering materials, and for supervising the work on the site. Due to his lack of skill in this respect, there are piles of excess materials on the site of a recently completed project. On the contract still uncompleted, much of the walls within the houses had to be knocked down, after having been built to roof level, because the chairman misread the plans and allowed the walls to be built without first inserting the door frames. Bad workmanship is also a feature of the work of this Co-operative. Some windows are set crooked, roofs are badly nailed on, etc. At present there is a building supervisor from the Federation of Building Societies on the site, but he spends most of the day in his caravan because of the aforementioned strike.

Materials

All materials, including concrete blocks but excluding sand and stone, come from either Kabwe or Lusaka. There is no co-operative making bricks locally.

Transport

Local transport can be hired from a local businessman to carry sand and stone. As far as materials from Lusaka and Kabwe are concerned, these are carried by either the transport belonging to the Federation or by public transport, such as Jukes Curtis Ltd.

Dividends

The dividends are decided by the committee on the advice of the chairman, who keeps the books. The members claim to have been paid only K40 every quarter and it appears obvious that most of the dividends have gone into the chairman's pockets. The chairman's whereabouts are at present unknown.

M. A. B. Christie

10 June 1970

C. Widstrand

Bibliographical Notes

Research into co-operative problems in East Africa has been carried out to a certain extent by the co-operatives themselves, but since the middle of the 'sixties it has also been carried out by other research organizations and universities. To the former category belongs the research into the economic and management problems, carried out, for example, by the *Co-operative Research Unit* of the Co-operative Development Division of the Ministry of Agriculture and Co-operatives in Dar-es-Salaam. Up to June 1971, five research papers had been published, on the coconut industry, rice-milling activities, the internal financing of co-operatives, rural credit and similar topics.

Research has also been carried out by the *Joint Research Project on Co-operatives,* which is sponsored by the Co-operative College, Co-operative Education Centre, Moshi, and the Economic Research Bureau, University of Dar-es-Salaam.

A. Kimario, C. C. Mtawali, H. Pedersen and Paul Westergaard have published a series of research papers dealing with the following subjects:

> *The Economic Performance in 1966–7 of the Primary Societies Affiliated to the KNCU* (Pedersen, Westergaard).
> *Co-operatives in Tanzania—Their Function as Economic and Democratic Institutions. Some Comments* (Westergaard, a revised version printed in Widstrand, 1970, pp. 121–152).
> *Inspection of Co-operative Societies* (Kimario, Pedersen).

The Development Planning Division of the Department of Co-operative Development has planned to do further work on the position of the personnel in the KNCU and to make an economic analysis of the KNCU and affiliated societies.

Some valuable reports have also been produced in the Co-operative Development Department in Nairobi, for example, an extensive study of graded staff in Kenyan co-operatives:

Survey of Graded Staff Employed by Co-operative Societies (July 1970, mimeo.).
Report of a Survey and a Refinding of Settlement Co-operative Societies (H. Aschiem, December 1968, mimeo.).

One of the main duties of the Department is to carry out basic district surveys and economic studies in the different districts of Kenya, such as

Kinangop Survey (Hannu Ikonen, March 1970, mimeo.) and
Economic Study and Recommendations on Co-operative Activities, Coast Province, Kilifi District (July 1971),

as well as various types of surveys of transport, vehicles, book-keeping procedures, etc.
The following are two basic and very important policy statements:

J. Nyerere's *Socialism and Rural Development* (Dar-es-Salaam 1967) and
K. Kaunda's *Address at the Opening of the National Co-operative Conference* at the Evelyn Hone College for Further Education in Lusaka, 12 January 1970.

Much valuable information can, of course, also be found in the reports of the various commissions of inquiry and government position papers, as well as the annual reports of the Registrars and the Departments or Divisions of Co-operatives:

Kenya
Kenya Government, *Co-operative Development Policy for Kenya,* Sessional Paper No. 8, 1970.

Registrar of Co-operative Societies, *Annual Reports.*

Department of Co-operative Development, *Annual Reports,* 1960, 1961, 1962.

Tanzania

The United Republic of Tanzania, *Proposals of the Tanzanian Government on the Recommendations of the Special Presidential Committee of Enquiry into Co-operative Movement and Marketing Boards* (Government Paper No. 3 of 1966).

Report of the Presidential Special Committee of Enquiry into Co-operative Movement and Marketing Boards. Dar-es-Salaam, 1966.

The United Republic of Tanzania, *Annual Reports of the Ministry of Co-operatives and Commerce,* Dar-es-Salaam.

The United Republic of Tanzania, *Annual Reports of the Ministry of Agriculture and Co-operatives,* Dar-es-Salaam 1970.

The United Republic of Tanzania, Ministry of Agriculture, Food and Co-operatives, Co-operative Development Division, *Note on the Co-operative Movement in Tanzania,* Dar-es-Salaam, September 1969.

Uganda

Uganda Protectorate, *Commission of Inquiry into the Coffee Industry,* Entebbe 1957.

Uganda Protectorate, *Report of the Commission of Inquiry into the Bugisu Coffee Industry,* Entebbe 1958.

Uganda Protectorate, *Government Memorandum on the Future Organization of the Bugisu Coffee Industry, Sessional Paper No. 19, 1958.*

Uganda Protectorate, *Report of the Commission of Inquiry into the Cotton Ginning Industry of Uganda,* Entebbe 1962.

Uganda Government, *Report of the Official Committee of Inquiry into the Busoga Growers' Co-operative Union, Ltd.,* Entebbe 1965.

Uganda Government, *Report of the Committee of Inquiry into the Cotton Industry,* Entebbe 1966.

Uganda Government, *The Report of the Committee of*

Inquiry into the Affairs of All Co-operative Unions in Uganda (Avaisa Report), Entebbe 1967.

Republic of Uganda, *Government White Paper on the Report of the Committee of Inquiry into the Coffee Industry, Sessional Paper No. 3, 1968.*

Uganda Government, Department of Co-operative Development, *Annual Reports.*

Mauritius

Mauritius Government, Department of Co-operation, *Annual Report.*

Zambia

Zambia Government, Department of Co-operatives, *Annual Report.*

From the Institute of Development Studies at the University of Nairobi have come several studies on various aspects of co-operatives. Professor Göran Hydén has written a book on the Kenyan co-operatives with the provisional title *African Co-operatives: A Study of Organizational Management in Rural Kenya,* published in 1971 by the O.U.P., Nairobi. He has also contributed to several other volumes mentioned here. Edward Karanja, who has worked together with Dr. Hydén, has also been working on co-operative problems. His latest report is called *The Problems of Amalgamating Co-operative Societies: The Case of Northern Tetu* (IDS Staff Paper No. 97, April 1971) and is included in this volume.

At the University of Dar-es-Salaam, research into co-operatives and into the *Ujamaa* movement has been undertaken in several departments. Several field reports on various *Ujamaa* villages have been issued by the Rural Development Research Committee from 1968 onwards. D. and R. Feldman have published *Co-operation and the Production Environment* (Economic Research Bureau Paper No. 69.12; similar versions published in Colin Ley's *Politics and Change in Developing Countries* (C.U.P. 1969) and as Rural Research Paper No. 100 (Kampala 1970).

From the Department of Political Science have come several

B.A. dissertations on co-operatives, for example, Shem Migot Adholla's *The Politics of a Growers' Co-operative Society* (Dar-es-Salaam 1969), J. S. D. Mwaikambo's *Kagwina Coffee Growers Society* (Dar-es-Salaam 1969), and C. M. Nyirabu's *The Role of Co-operatives in Agricultural Marketing in Eastern Mara* (Dar-es-Salaam 1970). Under the title of *Building Ujamaa Villages in Tanzania* (University of Dar-es-Salaam, Studies in Political Science No. 2, Tanzania Publishing House, Dar-es-Salaam 1971), J. H. Proctor has edited the following political-science dissertations:

I. K. S. Musoke, *Building Socialism in Bukoba: The Establishment of Rugazi (Nyerere) Ujamaa Village*
B. B. Bakula, *The Effect of Traditionalism on Rural Development: The Omurunazi Ujamaa Village, Bukoba*
E. N. Ntirukigwa, *The Land Tenure System and the Building of Ujamaa Villages in Geita: A Case Study of Kalbeezo*
A. W. M. Daraja, *The Tanzanian Pattern of Rural Development: Some Administrative Problems*
R. K. Mashauri, *Leadership Structure and Functions in an Ujamaa Village: A Case Study of Gallu*
G. R. Mboya, *The Feasibility of Ujamaa Villages in Kilimanjaro*

Three other volumes are the result of intensive research work into East African co-operatives. The first (*Social Prerequisites for Agricultural Co-operation*) is not yet published but is the result of a seminar held at the Institute of Development Studies at the University of Sussex in April 1969. The following papers were presented:

R. P. Dore, Traditional Communities and Modern Co-operatives
Percy S. Cohen, Modern Co-operatives and Traditional Societies
John S. Saul, Marketing Co-operatives in Tanzania
J. M. Texier, Traditional Forms of Collective Activities

In April 1970 the Scandinavian Institute of African Studies held a seminar at the University of Uppsala on the subject of

Co-operatives and Rural Development in East Africa. A volume with the same title has been edited by Carl G. Widstrand (Uppsala and New York 1970) and contains the following papers:

S. E. Migot-Adholla, Traditional Society and Co-operatives

Lionel Cliffe, Traditional *Ujamaa* and Modern Producer Co-operatives in Tanzania

Göran Hydén, Co-operatives and Their Socio-political Environment

J. P. W. B. McAuslan, Co-operatives and the Law in East Africa

Poul W. Westergaard, Co-operatives in Tanzania as Economic and Democratic Institutions

O. Okereke, The Place of Marketing Co-operatives in the Economy of Uganda

Nelson Kasfir, Organizational Analysis and Ugandan Co-operative Unions

Raymond Apthorpe, Some Problems of Evaluation

Carl Gösta Widstrand, Efficiency and Co-operatives

Dan Nyanjom, Some Observations on the Seminar on Co-operatives and Rural Development in East Africa

The United Nations Research Institute for Social Development has published a series on *Rural Institutions and Planned Change.* One of the volumes, edited by Raymond Apthorpe (Geneva 1970), is entitled *Rural Co-operatives and Planned Change in Africa: Case Materials* and contains the following papers:

M. Dravi, The Birth of Two Fishing Co-operatives in Ghana

FAO–UNRISD, Some Old and New Co-operative Experiences in Cameroon

E. A. Brett, Problems of Co-operative Development in Uganda

G. Hydén and E. Karanja, Co-operatives and Rural Development in Kenya

C. S. Lombard, Farming-co-operative Developments in Zambia and a Note on One Communal Society

A. Godart, Les unités de production agricole en Tunisie

N. Long, Co-operative Enterprise and Rural Development in Tanzania

There have been several international conferences dealing with agricultural co-operatives, such as the *Second Ad Hoc Consultation on Agricultural Co-operatives and Other Farmers' Associations in Africa* (held in Nairobi, June 1969) from which there is a *Report* (FAO, Rome 1970), mainly containing an impressive list of the names of the participants. At a conference in Moshi (October 1969) sponsored by the Economic Commission for Africa and the Dag Hammarskjöld Foundation and entitled *The Integrated Approach to Rural Development in Africa,* Dr. Göran Hydén gave a paper on the *Role of Co-operatives in Rural Development* (E/CN. M/SWCD/45).

Several German research workers have been interested in the development of East African co-operatives, for example, Margarete Paulus (*Das Genossenschaftswesen in Tanganyika und Uganda,* IFO Institut, Munich 1967). Furthermore, interesting studies on co-operative development in the developing countries have been carried out at the Institut für Genossenschaftswesen (Institute for Co-operation in Developing Countries), University of Marburg, under the direction of Professor E. Dülfer. A study on how to measure operational efficiency in co-operatives has been carried out in Kenya by J. Kuhn and H. Stoffregen (*How to Measure the Efficiency of Agricultural Co-operatives in Developing Countries,* Marburg/Lahn 1971). Hans H. Münkner, of the same Institute, has published *New Trends in Co-operative Law of English-Speaking Countries of Africa* (Marburg/Lahn 1971).

The 6th International Congress of Co-operative Science in 1969 was devoted to the subject of "Co-operatives in Economic Growth" and in the published report there are several relevant papers, for example, "The Role of Co-operatives in Developing Countries" by André Hirschfeld, Paris (*Zeitschrift für das Gesamte Genossenschaftswesen, Sonderheft,* "Co-operatives in Economic Growth", published by the Institute for Rural Co-operative Research at the Justus Liebig University, Giessen 1969).

Professor Guy Hunter is Director of the Joint Research Programme on Agricultural Development Overseas at the Overseas Development Institute, University of Reading. In a mimeographed *résumé,* he has made some relevant suggestions, which have been quoted in his paper *Research on Co-operatives Review Note* (March 1971).

Finally, at the International Co-operative Alliance headquarters in London there is a Secretary for Research (currently Mrs. L. Stettner). The Alliance tries to monitor all relevant co-operative research.

Notes

C. Widstrand, pp. 9–31

1. Nyerere, J., 1967, *Socialism and Rural Development.* Government Printer, Dar-es-Salaam, 1967.

2. Karanja, E., 1971, *The Problems of Amalgamating Co-operative Societies. The Case of Northern Tetu.* University of Nairobi, Institute of Development Studies, Staff Paper No. 97, Nairobi, April 1971.

3. Migot-Adholla, S., 1969, *Management Problems in a Co-operative Organization, The Case of the UFCU Tractor Project.* Mimeographed.

4. Feldman, D. and R., 1970, *Co-operation and the Production Environment.* Rural Development Research Paper No. 100, Kampala 1970. Mimeographed.

5. Musoke, I. K. S., 1970, "Building Socialism in Bukoba: The Establishment of Rugazi (Nyerere) *Ujamaa* Village", in Proctor, J. H. (ed.), *Building Ujamaa Villages in Tanzania.* University of Dar-es-Salaam, Studies in Political Science No. 2 (1971).

6. Hydén, G., 1971, *African Co-operatives: A Study of Organizational Management in Rural Kenya.* Nairobi, O.U.P. 1971.

7. Brett, E. D., 1970, *"Problems of Co-operative Development in Uganda",* in Apthorpe, R. (ed.), *Rural Co-operatives and Planned Change in Africa.* UNRISD, Geneva 1970, pp. 95–126.

8. Widstrand, C. G. (ed.), 1970, *Co-operatives and Rural Development in East Africa.* Scandinavian Institute of African Studies. Uppsala 1970.

9. Hunter, G., 1971, *Co-operatives: Effects of the Social Matrix.* Reading 1971. Mimeographed.

10. Mwaikambo, J. S. D., 1969, *Kagwina Coffee Growers' Society.* Department of Political Science, University of Dar-es-Salaam, 1969. Mimeographed undergraduate dissertation.

11. Nyirabu, C. M., 1970, *The Role of Co-operatives in Agricultural Marketing in Eastern North Mara.* Department of Political Science, University of Dar-es-Salaam, 1970, p. 32. Mimeographed undergraduate dissertation.

12. McHenry, D. C., 1969, *A Problem of Development: An Attempt to Form a Viable Fishermen's Co-operative Society for Lake Tanganyika.* Paper presented to the University of East Africa.

P. Nowrojee, pp. 62–80

1. The equivalent Kenyan provision, which is very similar, is Section 80 (1) and (2), Co-operative Societies Act, Cap. 490 (Act No. 39 of 1966). The equivalent Tanzanian provision is Section 99 (2) (*m*) of the Co-operative Societies Act, No. 27 of 1968, read together with Rule 22, The Co-operative Societies Rules, 1968 (G.N. 264/1968).

2. *Lukenya Ranching & Farming Co-operative Society Limited v. Kavoloto* (1970) E.A. 414 at 416.

3. *Wakiro v. Bugisu Co-operative Union* (1968) E.A. 523.

4. Ibid., at 527.

5. *Gatanga Coffee Growers' Co-operative Society Limited v. Gitau* (1970) E.A. 361.

6. *Kisanlal v. Co-operative Central Bank, Seoni* A.I.R. (1946) Nagpur 16.

7. See the Gatanga case, note 5 above.

8. I.L.R. (1938) 2 Calcutta 103 at 122.

9. Sastri, *The Law & Practise of Co-operative Societies in India,* Allahabad, New Book Co., 1968, 2nd ed., at 61.

10. See, for example, *Vinkar Mandal v. Narayana Rao Dabhade & Anor* A.I.R. (1948) Nagpur 327; *Belshill & Mossend Co-operative Society Ltd. v. Dalziel Co-operative Society Limited* (1960) 1 All E.R. 673.

11. See Göran Hydén, Co-operatives and their Socio-Political Environment, *Co-operatives and Rural Development in East Africa,* Uppsala, Scandinavian Institute of African Studies, 1970; Edward Karanja, A Case Study of Two Co-operatives in Kirinyaga, Nairobi, University College, I.D.S. Staff Paper No. 62; 'John Rajabu', Troubles Erupt in the Co-ops. *East Africa Journal,* June 1966; John Saul, Marketing Co-operatives in Tanzania, *Taamuli,* March 1971, Vol. 1, No. 2.

12. *Cox v. Hutchinson* (1910) 1 Ch. 513.

13. *Morrison v. Glover* (1849) 154 E.R. 1281.

14. *Kavoloto v. Lukenya Ranching & Farming Co-operative Society Ltd.* (Unreported Ruling, Mosdell J.) Nairobi H.C.C.C. 391 of 1966.

15. *Cox v. Hutchinson,* note 12 above.

16. *Albon v. Pyke* (1842) 4 M. & G. 421 at 425; followed in *Chite v. East African Community* (1970) E.A. 487.

17. *Crisp v. Bunbury* (1832) 131 E.R. 445.

18. Ibid.

19. *Smith v. Selwyn* (1914) 3 K.B. 98.

20. For fuller requirements, see H. H. Marshall, *Natural Justice,* Sweet & Maxwell, London 1959.

21. *Hira Nand v. Anjuman Bank* A.I.R. (1935) Lah. 631.

22. The Co-operative Societies Act has its source in Indian legislation (the *Gatanga* case) and in the Model Co-operative Societies Ordinance of the British Colonial Office.

23. *Lee v. Showmen's Guild* (1952) 2 Q.B. 329 at 354.

24. Göran Hydén, Government and Co-operatives, *Development Administration,* Ed. Hydén, Jackson and Okumu. Nairobi, O.U.P. 1970, pp. 304, 305.

25. John Saul, note 11 above, and S. E. Migot-Adholla, The Politics of a Growers' Co-operative Society, cited in Hydén above.

26. Franz C. Helm, *The Economics of Co-operative Enterprise,* London, Co-operative College, Moshi/Univ. of London Press, 1968, 234.

S. E. Migst-Adholla, pp. 81–104

1. See, for example, the suggested measures for efficiency in the AID study by Herbert C. Keriesel *et al.* (Agricultural Marketing in Tanzania, Background Research and Policy Proposals, USAID, June 1970).

2. No attempt is made in this paper to deal with the events which led to the re-organization of the VFCU into the NCU.

3. The term has been used by Raymond Apthorpe to refer to planners and administrators (see his "Golden Eggs of Agricultural Co-operatives", a paper presented at the Conference on the Social Pre-requisites for Agricultural Co-operation, Institute of Development Studies, University of Sussex, 31 March to 3 April 1969, p. 4).

4. It seems that the co-operative inspectors regarded their duties as the supervision of account books in respect of produce marketing. Although tractor records were also sent to the inspectorate for checking, almost no action was taken to correct the gross anomalies.

5. It would appear that the regulation against such practices was only half-heartedly enforced. A circular from the Regional Co-operative Office, Shinayanga, dated 9 February 1968, mentioned

that "It has been discovered that some departmental officers have been taking loans from the co-operative societies. This is bad practice, and it is illegal . . .".

6. This idea has been described by R. P. Dore in "Traditional Communities and Modern Co-operatives", a paper presented at the Conference on the Social Pre-requisites for Agricultural Co-operation, Institute of Development Studies, University of Sussex, 31 March to 3 April 1969, pp. 5 ff.

7. It is not clear what use was made of these statistics (see Tables 1–6). No effort was made to calculate ratios as measures of performance. See, for an example of such ratios, H. E. Larzade and R. M. King, *Ratios as Measuring Sticks for Elevator and Farm Supply Organisations,* Michigan State University, Agricultural Experiment Station, Department of Agricultural Economics, Special Bulletin No. 360, August 1952; an example is also included in Franz C. Helm, *The Economics of Co-operative Enterprise,* University of London Press, 1968.

8. For an account of the early history of the co-operative movement, see Andrew Meguire, *Towards Uhuru in Tanzania: The Politics of Participation,* Cambridge University Press, Cambridge, 1969.

9. "Tractors . . . have been commandeered by Regional and Area Commissioners and operated at substantial losses for the benefit of non-co-operative schemes, sometimes, for example, being required to be used on TANU Youth Farms without charge" (*Report of Presidential Committee of Inquiry into Co-operative Movement and Marketing Boards,* Government Printers, Dar-es-Salaam 1966, p. 71).

10. Complete report of the research on which this paper is based was submitted for the B.A. degree in Political Science at University College, Dar-es-Salaam (see S. E. Migot-Adholla, The Politics of a Growers' Co-operative Society, unpublished dissertation, University College, Dar-es-Salaam, March 1969). A revised version of this paper is to be published in a volume by L. R. Cliffe, W. L. Luttrell, S. E. Migot-Adholla and J. S. Saul entitled *Towards Rural Co-operation in Tanzania* (forthcoming).

E. Karanja, pp. 105–133

1. Republic of Kenya, *Development Plan 1970–74,* p. 277. Government Printer, Nairobi.

2. Sessional Paper No. 8 of 1970, Co-operative Development Policy for Kenya, p. 2. Government Printer, Nairobi.

3. Göran Hydén, *African Co-operatives: A Study of Organizational Management in Rural Kenya,* p. 213 (in press).

4. James D. Thompson and William J. McEmen, "Organizational Goals and Environment" in Etziani (ed.), *Complex Organizations,* p. 186.

5. G. Hydén and E. Karanja, "Co-operatives and Rural Development in Kenya", in R. J. Apthorpe (ed.), *Rural Co-operatives and Planned Change in Africa,* UNRISD, Vol. IV, p. 208. Geneva 1970.

6. Göran Hydén, op. cit., p. 81.

7. C. G. Widstrand (ed.), *Co-operatives and Rural Development in East Africa,* p. 242. Africana Publishing Corporation, New York, 1970.

8. Ibid., p. 238.

9. David H. Pickard, "Factors Affecting Success and Failure in Farmers' Co-operative Associations", *Journal of Agricultural Economics,* Vol. XXI, No. 1, January 1970.

10. Ibid.

11. Hydén and Karanja, op. cit., p. 205.

12. Sessional Paper, op. cit., p. 3.

13. J. A. E. Morley, "The State of Agricultural Co-operation in Its Centenary Year", *Journal of Agricultural Economics,* Vol. XIX, No. 1, January 1968.

14. See Republic of Kenya, Development Plan 1970–74, p. 276.

15. Göran Hydén, "Co-operatives and Their Socio-Political Environment" in C. G. Widstrand, op. cit., p. 62.

16. G. Solomon, "Land Reform and the Promotion of Small-Scale Industries and Services through Rural Multi-Purpose Co-operatives", *Land Reform: Land Settlement and Co-operatives,* FAO No. 1, 1970, p. 89.

17. See Franz C. Helm, *The Economics of Co-operative Enterprise,* p. 106. University of London Press 1968.

18. Hydén, op. cit., p. 184.

19. Ibid., p. 75.

20. Kurt R. Anschel, Russell A. Brannon and Eldon D. Smith (eds.), *Agricultural Co-operatives and Markets in Developing Countries,* p. 209. Frederick Prager, New York 1969.

21. C. G. Widstrand (ed.), op. cit., p. 239.